James Cowe

Religious and Philanthropic Tracts

James Cowe

Religious and Philanthropic Tracts

ISBN/EAN: 9783337131173

Printed in Europe, USA, Canada, Australia, Japan

Cover: Foto ©Lupo / pixelio.de

More available books at **www.hansebooks.com**

RELIGIOUS

AND

PHILANTHROPIC

TRACTS:

CONSISTING OF

1. A Difcourfe on the Principles, the Temper, and Duties of Chriftians; the fecond Edition, enlarged:
2. An Effay on the State of the Poor, and on the Means of improving it by Friendly Societies, &c.
3. Rules for forming and managing Friendly Societies, with a View to facilitate their general Eftablifhment.

By *JAMES COWE*, M.A.
VICAR OF SUNBURY, MIDDLESEX.

———————————*Alterius fic*
Altera pofcit opem res, et conjurat amicè.   Hor.

LONDON:

PRINTED FOR J. ROBSON, NEW BOND-STREET;
F. AND C. RIVINGTON, ST. PAUL'S CHURCH-YARD;
T. AND G. WILKIE, PATER-NOSTER-ROW;
AND D. BREMNER, STRAND.

1697.

The following Difcourfe was originally printed for the ufe of the Author's Parifhioners, and only the fubftance of it delivered from the pulpit, at an anniverfary meeting of two Friendly Societies of poor tradefmen and day-labourers at Sunbury, inftituted for their mutual fupport in cafes of ficknefs, accident, or old age.

In the Effay, many of the caufes, which have combined to deprefs the underftandings, and increafe the miferies of the lower claffes of fociety, are ftated——Proper means of inftruction, improvement, and relief, fuggefted.——The beneficial effects of the Friendly Societies at Sunbury in reducing the poor-rates, and the importance of fuch focieties to the public, as the means of preventing poverty, elucidated.—With obfervations on Female Benefit-Clubs.

ON THE PRINCIPLES, THE TEMPER,

AND

DUTIES OF CHRISTIANS.

PHILIPPIANS, i. 27.

Only let your conversation be as becometh the Gospel of Christ.

THE Gospel of Christ has produced a very wonderful change in the condition and sentiments of every nation, where its sacred truths have been received. It has given the most sublime views of God and his Providence, of human nature, and of a future state. It has made known what we are to believe concerning the Father, the Son, and the Holy Ghost, in the stupendous work of man's redemption. It has revealed this momentous truth,

truth, that "eternal life is the gift of God, through Jesus Christ our Lord." It has exhibited the most astonishing display of the Divine goodness, in raising a whole race of intelligent beings from a state of ignorance and vice, and in conducting them, if it be not their own fault, through a scene of trial and moral discipline, to the highest degree of improvement and felicity, of which their nature is susceptible. To this great end, it has taught us, in the plainest manner, the important duties we owe to God, to our neighbour, and to ourselves. It has commanded us to love and fear God, to worship and serve him with a pure and pious heart; to cultivate justice and benevolence to our neighbour, and sobriety and temperance with regard to ourselves. It has impressed this awful truth, that the disposition of the mind is what God principally regards; and it has informed us, that his Holy Spirit will influence our minds, and co-operate with our sincere endeavours in the discharge of our duty, and in enabling us to act according to the great principles of our religion. It has shewn us the efficacy of repentance, and on what

what terms we may obtain the remiffion of fins. It has alfo given us fome important difcoveries of the condition of good and bad men in a future ftate, and points out the intimate relation which this life bears to the next. In a word, the Gofpel records the birth, the life, the miracles, the death, and refurrection,—the doctrines and precepts, of the Son of God; and it contains that Divine fyftem of religion revealed in the New Teftament, which has been, and, we doubt not, will continue to be, the means of beftowing virtue and happinefs on millions of our fellow-creatures.

These are fome of the leading *doctrines* of Chriftianity, which have a tendency to increafe every real and genuine enjoyment of profperity, and can hardly fail to animate the virtuous heart, and fupport it amidft the various afflictions incident to human nature. And, in endeavouring to illuftrate the exhortation of the Apoftle, and in applying it to the purpofe of our prefent meeting, we fhall have occafion to take notice of, and inculcate

culcate some of the benevolent *precepts* which it enjoins.

The text requires that you should be actuated in your personal deportment, and in your intercourse with society, by the precepts and laws of Christianity, and necessarily directs us to the consideration of its *practical* truths. " Only let your conversation be as " becometh the Gospel of Christ *."

Now,

---

* *Only behave worthy of the Gospel of Christ.* Πολιτευεσθε literally denotes, that ye behave as denizens, or freemen of some city or civil polity. The expression is evidently borrowed from the conduct of good citizens, who act suitably to the laws of the community of which they are members. The same expression occurs ch. iii. 20. Ἡμων γαρ το ΠΟΛΙΤΕΥΜΑ εν ουρανοις ὑπαρχει. The meaning of which will be best understood, by comparing it with what the Apostle says in the preceding verse, where he speaks of those who spend their lives merely in sensual gratifications, and only " mind earthly things." But, as Christians, " *our* conversation," says he, Ἡμων το πολιτευμα, " is in Heaven." Our thoughts and affections, our hopes and desires, are all directed to the attainment of future happiness. In our sentiments, in our actions,

Now, to explain and recommend this duty, which, in the judgment of the Apostle, appeared so reasonable and important, I shall, first, consider what ought to be the rule of your conduct towards mankind in general: secondly, what particular duties the Gospel requires of men who live in the same city or neighbourhood: thirdly, how you ought to behave towards those who differ from you in religious opinions: fourthly, how you should conduct yourselves in your respective families: and, lastly, I shall point out those duties which you owe to each other, as the members of Friendly Societies, and shall state how their interests may be best promoted.

actions, and "conversation," we are governed by the Heavenly principles and laws of our religion. While we conduct ourselves as inhabitants of this earth, and endeavour to be good and useful members of civil society, we recollect that we are immortal beings, subjects of the moral government of God, and hope, by the discoveries and mercies which Christianity affords, to be at last admitted into the society of the blessed above—" *the* " *City of the living God.*" Heb. xii. 22, and xiii. 14. So that the text, thus far explained, opens a wide field of duty and enquiry: *Only behave as becomes those to whom the Gospel of Christ is revealed.*

These are topics of the greatest importance, highly necessary to be enforced in times, wherein the benefits arising from society seem not sufficiently attended to; and if, in discussing them, and in shewing their influence on your behaviour and "conversation," this discourse should exceed our usual limits, your patience and attention must be entreated.—
Let us, then,

I. Consider the principles of the Gospel with regard to mankind in general. Man is a social being; the instinct of his nature impels him to apply to his fellow-creatures for protection and security, and for the endearments of friendly intercourse. Our wants and our wishes shew that we are connected by the sacred tie of humanity. This law is so deeply impressed on our minds by the hand of our Creator, that we must stifle the finest feelings of nature, if we allow ourselves to cherish animosity or envy, and are not inclined to justice and charity. Deprived of the comforts of society, and of all intercourse of sentiment, what miserable and forlorn

forlorn creatures should we be! Accustomed to enjoy the blessings of civil and religious liberty, our condition would be far more wretched, than if we had never known the pleasures of social life, or the advantages of regular government. By society, however, and by the influence of Christianity, the ferocity of human nature is diminished, and even the horrors of war and the rage of persecution are mitigated. The manners and the laws of mankind are evidently softened and improved; and we can trace a gradual advancement in civilization *, in virtue, and in religion. When the Gospel was first published, servants were slaves; but, under the mild and benevolent spirit of Christianity, servitude has been so much softened, and the human heart so far enlarged, that no one can *now*

---

* If it should be thought, that this is hardly applicable to the condition of such societies as consist of poor tradesmen and day-labourers, let it be remarked, that some of the author's hearers are friends and promoters of these excellent institutions; and their education, their manners, and their habits, are so many proofs of the principles here adduced.

be

be at a loss to know, " who is his neighbour." We all know that we have one common nature, and that every man is to be considered as our neighbour, whom we are able to assist. By acts of kindness, and by our endeavours to suppress vice and misery, and to diffuse virtue and happiness among mankind, we resemble the greatest and the best of Beings; and, according to our abilities, become " merciful, as our Father, who is in heaven, is merciful."—Such is the general principle of benevolence, which evinces that man is designed by his Maker for society, and should maintain a mutual intercourse of good offices, in order that his " conversation may be as becometh the Gos-
" pel of Christ."—Let us,

II. Consider those particular duties, which Christianity requires of men who live in the same city or neighbourhood. Now, the law of humanity, which, you see, extends to the whole human race, will be found to operate more powerfully, when applied to those who are united into one community, and associate for mutual comfort and protection. Though Christianity requires

requires us to venerate the rights, and to feel for the sufferings, of all our fellow-creatures, yet it enjoins a particular attachment to the welfare and interest of those, with whom we are more intimately connected, either by kindred, by friendship, or by neighbourhood. Instead of confounding order and subordination, it clearly ascertains the rights of every individual. In every station and occupation of life, from the king on the throne to the peasant in the field, there are certain obvious duties enjoined by our religion; and happy would it be for every rank and condition of men, if they more commonly produced their genuine effects! In our transactions with each other, the doctrines of Christianity teach us to guard against injustice, violence, and fraud, and to cultivate veracity, probity, and benevolence. Men, in the higher ranks of society, should relieve distress, encourage industry, and promote virtue and religion. On the other hand, those who are placed by Providence in the lower stations of life should be honest, industrious, and orderly. All should be candid, peaceable, and kindly-affectioned one towards another.

other. By the exertion of our bodily strength, or by the energy of our minds, we should all endeavour to diffuse social happiness, and should never forget, whatever may be our circumstances in life, That we are fellow-creatures, liable to the same wants and infirmities, children of the same Heavenly Father, and, through his mercy in Christ Jesus, candidates for the same state of eternal felicity.

In your intercourse with society, you should particularly attend to that evangelical law, which cannot be too deeply engraved on your hearts, and—"*do to others as you would have them do to you.*" For, if men were always actuated by this great and general rule of Christianity, which is so important and so easily understood, they would never violate the peace of society, nor bring on themselves the reproach of injustice or inhumanity. On the contrary, they would feel that the first duty which they owe to others, is to do them no harm; and the next, to do them all the good they are able. Many imagine, because they are in indigent circumstances, that they have it not in their power to be charitable. But this is a mistake. In the daily commerce of life, you have frequent opportunities of doing good to your neighbour: you may speak well of him; you may vindicate his character if it has been unjustly defamed; you may give him friendly advice; you may comfort him in his afflictions; or, you may visit and assist him in sickness and distress. Surely all these are charitable acts; and the poorest, as well as the most opulent among us, cannot say that he is incapable of performing them. Wherever there is a real benevolence of temper, various methods will daily suggest themselves to you of being useful to each other; and, by this benignity of heart, you will give the most unequivocal proof of your religious sincerity: " By this shall all men "know that ye are Christ's disciples, if ye have love one to another." But among neighbours, and among men professing Christianity, this kind assistance is frequently withheld through envy, through hatred, through a selfish or contracted temper; and men foster those malignant passions, from which infinite mischief continually arises. Let me, therefore, intreat you to cherish an habitual tenderness and generosity of mind, and shew, by your

conduct

conduct and "conversation," that you are animated by that spirit of forgiveness and benevolence, which breathes in every page of the Gospel. You will thereby be good neighbours, and contribute your endeavours to sooth the afflictions of human life. God knows, the afflictions of life fall heavy upon all; and it is our interest, no less than our duty, to alleviate them as much as possible. And, if envy and strife, if ill-nature and detraction, if pride and discontent, were banished from the heart, some of the greatest calamities which men undergo would be removed. For, human misery proceeds, not so much from (what we call) the events of fortune, or the pains of the body, as from the turbulence of the passions, and the agitations of the mind.—Let us,

III. Consider how you ought to behave towards those who differ from you in religious opinions. In this imperfect state, where mankind possess different degrees of knowledge and capacity, it is in vain to expect an uniformity of sentiment. Nor does religion require it: while men do not propagate principles

ciples subversive of virtue and of peace, and repugnant to those eternal laws, which are imprinted on our minds by the great Author of order and of excellence, every man has an unalienable right to follow his own judgment, and, with candour and charity, to use those faculties for acquiring knowledge and truth, which Providence has bestowed on him. If we claim this privilege ourselves, we ought not to refuse it to others. Remember then, that no differences in religious tenets, should ever be the cause of intolerance, or should hinder you from treating other denominations of Christians with candour and forbearance. Remember, that violent disputes about religion, would be peculiarly improper among men who have not had the advantages of learning, and are, therefore, not so able to investigate some of the great truths, which the Gospel has revealed. Guard, then, against all party-rancour, which tends only to alienate the affections of Christians from one another; and be thankful, that you live in an age, when the rights of human nature are better known and maintained, and in a country, where every man is allowed the free and unmolested profession of his religion, according to the dictates of his conscience. Happy had it been for mankind, if this moderation had always subsisted in the Christian Church ; and if all who had professed Christianity, had regulated their temper and " conversation" according to its liberal and benevolent principles ! We are exhorted to contend earnestly for the faith ; but, let it ever be in the spirit of meekness, and of Christian charity ; for passion and intolerance, so far from advancing the cause of true religion, tend only to obstruct and disgrace it.—Let us,

IV. Consider how you should behave in your respective families, how the principles of the Gospel will operate in the regulation of your tempers, and of your domestic concerns. To this subject you should pay the greater attention, as many, who are regular in their profession of religion at church, are shamefully remiss in the duties of private life. Now, the first duty of every head of a family is, to promote a sense of religion in his own house. Family-prayer has a tendency to

maintain

maintain a spirit of devotion, to repress animosities, to increase benevolence, and to improve our virtue. And, as so many good consequences result from it, you should not fail to make it a part of your daily employment. If you allow the business of life to engage your whole attention; if it prevent you from devoting a small portion of your time, every day, to prayer to God; a period is fast approaching when you will acknowledge, with regret, that you were too deeply engaged in the pursuits of this world, and too inattentive to the concerns of the next. "O come," then, "let us worship and bow down, and kneel before the Lord our Maker. Worship him in the beauty of holiness *." Cultivate that elevation of mind, that reverence of Almighty God, that purity of heart, and integrity of life, which will shew the sincerity of your religious principles, and that your behaviour is "such as becometh the Gospel of Christ."

A second duty, to which, as Christians, you must particularly attend, is industry.

---

* Psalm xcvi. 9.

Man was never designed to be inactive: some are destined to procure their daily subsistence by the labour of their hands; and others, by the exertions of their minds. All are to be employed in some virtuous and useful occupation, suitable to their station and abilities. You are enjoined in Scripture " to be quiet, " and to do your own business, and to work " with your own hands *," at your respective employments. And, in another place, the Apostle expresses himself in still stronger language: " If any will not work, neither " should he eat †," and thereby become a burden on the industry of others. Now, if any of *you* were to neglect your business, and to spend your time in idleness or vice, the consequence would be very fatal to yourselves, and to your families. But, by virtuous industry, and by becoming members of Friendly Societies, you shew an independence of sentiment, and a principle of benevolence, which you should ever retain. I need not, therefore, expatiate on the ignominy and degradation of applying for parochial relief

* 1 Thess. iv. 11.   † 2 Thess. iii. 10.

without abſolute neceſſity, nor point out to you, how mean and unprincipled it is in men to live on the property and induſtry of others, when, by diligence and prudence, they might have ſupported themſelves, and avoided all the miſery and humiliation of a pariſh-maintenance. As long as you are induſtrious, and attentive to the duties of your ſtation, you will be reſpected; and, remember, while you are thus employed, you are fulfilling the wiſe purpoſes of Providence, and are promoting your eternal intereſts, even while you ſeem wholly engaged about the concerns of the preſent life.

A duty, nearly connected with induſtry, and highly conſiſtent with your Chriſtian principles, is frugality. Unleſs men pay attention to the management of their domeſtic concerns, they muſt inevitably fall into diſorder. And, as this will be found to be true, even in the ſuperior ranks of life, ſurely thoſe, whom I am now particularly addreſſing, muſt be ſenſible, that, without ſome prudence and care, *they* may ſoon be involved in embarraſſments and expences, from which it would

be almost impossible to extricate themselves. Many of the poor are extremely improvident in the management of their slender property, and aggravate their afflictions by their want of œconomy and foresight when they are young, and have no family to support. Instead of making any provision against accidental difficulties, they meanly depend upon parish maintenance, and unthinkingly squander in health, what might have supported them with comfort in sickness, or in age. —Your prudence, therefore, and your foresight, cannot be too highly commended, for appropriating part of your wages for your mutual support in cases of accident or of illness, somewhat resembling the custom which prevailed among the primitive Christians, of " assisting *their* poor brethren, and distribut-
" ing to every man according as his necessi-
" ties required *." By this means, if you happen, at any time, to be disabled by disease, or bowed down with the infirmities of Nature, you can apply to your Society for relief, and will be supported by a fund,

---
* Acts iv. 32—35.

which your own industry and œconomy have contributed to raise *.

That your moral and religious conduct may be "suitable to the Gospel," there is another domestic virtue which must not be omitted, and that is temperance. The great number of public-houses, and the disorderly manner in which many of them are kept, are no less detrimental to society, than destructive to religion. But, if you have any regard to decency and character; if you have any affection for your families, who naturally look up to you for protection and support; you will not quit the paths of sobriety and peace, and leave them a helpless prey to misery and want. By intemperance and excess, you im-

* It were much to be wished, that those, who are in the lower ranks of life, would all follow the same example in the season of youth, and become members of Amicable Societies, formed for such useful purposes. If these benevolent institutions could be made general, they would render parochial relief unnecessary; and would furnish a far more comfortable, and more honourable, support for the poor, than the present legal provision. This is strikingly evinced in the following Essay.

pair your health and your underftanding, you wafte your time and your fubftance, you ruin your families, and injure your morals. Drunkennefs is incompatible with a Chriftian life and " converfation ;" it is repugnant to that felf-government and purity, which the Gofpel requires you to cultivate, and is exprefsly mentioned among thofe vices, which will exclude you " from the kingdom of " God *." Againft a habit, then, fo pernicious to your happinefs, both here and hereafter, you can never be fufficiently guarded. Avoid, therefore, as far as poffible, the fociety and " converfation" of the idle, the profligate, and the drunken; and affociate with the induftrious, the virtuous, and the fober.

There is one duty more, deferving particular attention, which remains to be mentioned here; it is, that of promoting mutual affection, and gentlenefs of manners, in your refpective families. Of the fad effects of quarrels and diffenfions in private life, we

* Gal. v. 21.

have

have many melancholy proofs. In the very first age of the world, and among Adam's own sons, we have an awful instance of the dreadful consequence of variance and strife among relations. We find, that Cain entirely stifled his affection for his brother Abel; allowed the rancour of hatred and envy to take full possession of his heart; and at last, with impious hands, became his assassin.—When those, who are connected by the nearest and dearest ties of Nature, once acquire the habit of wrangling and disputing, all their domestic comforts are at an end, their tempers become soured, their peace of mind is ruined;—and thus, by their conduct and " conversation," they too evidently shew, that they are *not* " acting as becometh the " Gospel of Christ."

It was, therefore, the observation of the wise man, " Better is a dinner of herbs, " where love is, than a stalled ox, and " hatred therewith *." The most scanty or the most homely fare, accompanied with domestic harmony and peace, and with the love of God and virtue, is far

* Prov. xv. 17.

more delicious to the taste, and more pleasing to the mind, than the most splendid entertainment, imbittered by discord and strife, by profaneness and vice. You cannot, then, be too careful to regulate your tempers; to promote social affection, good-humour, and cheerfulness of " conversation" in your families; and to instil the same Christian principles into the minds of your children.—This leads me to some reflexions on their education, with a view that *they* may " behave as becometh the Gospel."

Among some weak and ill-informed minds an opinion has prevailed, that the lower orders of society should be kept in ignorance, and should not enjoy the benefit of education. The reason they assign is this: The poor, by education, become turbulent and inattentive to their business, and make a bad use of their knowledge. Now, admitting this to be sometimes the case, (for it is too obvious to be always denied,) it only shews, that the greatest blessings are liable to be perverted to the worst purposes; but it would be absurd to argue from thence against every improvement in science, in morals, and in religion. The truth is, it is not owing to Christianity, but to the want of it, that such grounds of complaint do arise. For, wherever a diffusion of true Christian knowledge has taken place, wherever its genuine principles are inculcated and received, there men will be sober, honest, industrious, peaceable, contented, and pious. But, when its duties are neglected, its sanctions unknown, and its obligations disregarded, then every principle, hostile to the peace, the interests, and the happiness of society, will be disseminated.

This shews you the importance of religious education, and the utility of Sunday schools. Of the utility, indeed, of these excellent institutions I have so often spoken, and you now seem so fully convinced, that it will be unnecessary for me to say much in their behalf. Among other advantages, you see that your children are thereby rescued from ignorance and depravity, are instructed in the great and fundamental doctrines of the Christian religion, and acquire settled habits of piety and virtue. They are accustomed to spend the

Sunday

Sunday in a proper manner, and are taught the moſt ſublime truths;—the neceſſity of living " ſoberly, righteouſly, and godly," in this world, that they may be uſeful members of ſociety, and make this life a paſſage to a better. You know, alſo, that they are at a critical period, when their minds are ready to receive any impreſſion, and when their future conduct and happineſs will, in a great meaſure, depend on the habits they now acquire. If pains be taken to train them up in the paths of innocence, virtue, and religion, there is reaſon to hope that, in mature age, they will not depart from them. But if they be once habituated to vice, and their " converſation" be contrary to the principles of the Goſpel, they, probably, will never abandon thoſe pernicious practices, but, by profligacy and wickedneſs, will bring down your " grey hairs with ſorrow to the grave." To guard againſt conſequences which are ſo fatal, you ſhould continue to ſend your children regularly to the Sunday-ſchools, and be thankful for the advantages thence derived — advantages which *you* did not enjoy

enjoy at the same period of your own lives *.

You should also pay great attention to their health and cleanliness †, and to their natural dispositions as they advance in life; and should restrain in them every violent passion, and every propensity to ill-nature, slander, and malevolence. Teach them, I beseech you, to be sober, chaste,

---

* It is only doing justice to my Parishioners to mention, that, from the highest down to those who receive benefit from the Sunday-schools, there is hardly an individual, who does not subscribe cheerfully and liberally to their support. And it is with singular pleasure I here observe, that, at present, they are in a very flourishing condition, and that their utility begins every day to be more sensibly felt. They require, however, constant attention, and a degree of prudence in their management, far greater than is generally imagined.

† This regard to cleanliness is attended with more important and beneficial consequences, than at first may be imagined. The state of the body is, in general, a true indication of the state of the mind. Rags and filth are the usual symptoms of idleness, improvidence, and vice: whereas habitual cleanliness not only contributes to health, but leads to that sanctity of heart, and purity of manners, which prepare men for a higher state of existence.

and

and honest; to be attentive to their promises and engagements, and content with their station. Inspire them with a detestation of lying, artifice, and theft; and train them up to the early habits of cheerful industry, and to the regular practice of every social and moral obligation. But, above all, endeavour to impress on their young minds a deep sense of Religion, and of the duties they owe to their God and Saviour. Often remind them, that, though their earthly master may be absent, yet they are under the constant inspection of their *Heavenly* Master, to whom we are all accountable.

These are very essential duties, which you should not fail to inculcate as far as you are able; and if some of you can give but little instruction in the way of precept, you can all be useful in a still higher degree—*by setting them a good example.* This is a duty peculiarly incumbent on every one who stands in the important and endearing relation of a parent. I must particularly admonish you, then, to let your general "conversation," and your whole deportment, correspond with the principles of the Religion which you profess.

If

If you endeavour to give them good advice, and a good example, you have little elfe to bequeath to them. Nor do they want more: while they enjoy the bleffing of health, they can always maintain themfelves by their perfonal labour: and, if unavoidable afflictions befal them, they will, no doubt, meet with affiftance and relief from the charitable and well-difpofed. You have, therefore, no reafon to be folicitous about them after they are grown up; in this refpect you enjoy an advantage over the higher claffes of fociety—over thofe whom you are apt to envy, and to think fo happy. *They* have often great anxiety about their children; they are not always able to give them a fortune fuited to their rank and expectations, nor can they eafily determine what profeffion to choofe for them. Now, this is a perplexity from which *you* are exempted. Providence difpenfes happinefs among the human race with a far more equal hand than a fuperficial obferver is willing to allow. By the fimplicity of your lives, and the tranquillity of your habitations, you enjoy that health of body, and that ferenity of mind, frequently unknown

to

to the opulent and the great. So that, when you think of the comforts you want, you should reflect alfo on the anxieties and temptations from which you are free, and on the bleffings, both civil and religious, which you enjoy. If you are attentive to the duties of your humble, but important, ftation, and take care that your children do not acquire bad habits, you will, in the decline of life, derive unfpeakable confolation in reflecting, that you ufed your beft endeavours to regulate their paffions, and to form their minds to piety and virtue; and, when the folemn period of your diffolution draweth nigh, "this will be your rejoicing—The teftimony "of your confciences, that, in fimplicity and "godly fincerity, not with carnal wifdom, "but with the grace of God, you have had "your converfation in the world*." You will then be fupported by God's prefence, at a feafon moft awful to human nature, and may commit your offspring to the care of that gracious Providence, who hath faid, "Leave thy fatherlefs children, I will pre-

---

* 2 Cor. i. 12.

" ferve them alive; and let thy widows truft
" in me *."

Having thus ftated, at fome length, the duties which you owe in your refpective families, and having particularly dwelt on the neceffity of attending to the education and behaviour of your children—a topic fo important in its nature, and which might be made fo beneficial in its confequences,—I now proceed, in the laft place,

V. To point out thofe duties which you owe to one another as the members of Friendly Societies, and to fhew how their interefts may be beft promoted. This is partly anticipated by what has been already advanced; I fhall, however, fuggeft a few general obfervations, which, if attended to, may this day be ufeful to you.

The Pfalmift felt much pleafure in feeing men live in amity and peace. "Behold," fays he, "how good and pleafant it is for "brethren to dwell together in unity." It diffufes a fpirit of benevolence through all

---

* Jeremiah, xlix. 11.

ranks, and unites them in one bond of mutual interest, and of social affection. You will, therefore, at all times, study to live in harmony and peace with your neighbours, cultivating a benevolent disposition towards all, and endeavouring to disseminate it among others. Were mankind always guided in their conduct and "conversation" by the heavenly principles and motives of the Gospel, what a change would take place in the world! " Nation would no longer lift up " their sword against nation, neither would " they learn war any more*." No turbulent spirit would attempt to interrupt the peace of society, or to invade the rights of individuals. All the animosities, which are occasioned by the jarring interests of men, would be suppressed; cheerfulness and contentment would animate every breast.

But this, alas! is far from being the present state of society; and, therefore, I cannot too earnestly guard you against those bitter animosities and civil dissensions, which so unhappily prevail. Without laws and subor-

---

* Isaiah, ii. 4.

dination

dination no society can long subsist. While the laws, or standing rules, of any community are revered and obeyed, its affairs will prosper; but, when they are despised and subverted, its interests will be neglected, and confusion will inevitably ensue. Among nations, tumult and faction always lead to rapine and violence, to anarchy and every species of outrage: and many a rich and flourishing society has been entirely ruined, when the spirit of discord and variance has once prevailed among the members. The benevolent Friend of man has, therefore, particularly warned us against civil commotions and intestine divisions. " Every kingdom, " divided against itself, is brought to desolation; and every city or house, divided against " itself, cannot stand *."

Of the truth of this divine remark, examples might be given from the history of every nation that has existed in the world; but, without adverting to the records of antiquity, the proceedings of your own societies will sufficiently evince its importance.

---

* Matthew, xii. 25.

When harmony and regularity subsist among you; when your behaviour, at all your meetings, is influenced by the principles, and regulated by the laws, of Christianity; then your societies will flourish, and you may humbly hope for that blessing of Heaven, that "*peace of God*," which can alone secure your social happiness, and domestic tranquillity. Earnestly, therefore, implore his sacred influence to enable you to act, at all times, as " becometh the Gospel;" and let me exhort you, in the words of the Apostle, and by the name of our Divine Master, to endeavour, as a society of men and of Christians, to promote mutual forbearance and good-humour, and to avoid quarrels and contentions. " I
" beseech you, brethren, by the name of our
" Lord Jesus Christ, that ye all speak the
" same thing, and that there be no divisions
" among you; but that ye be perfectly uni-
" ted in the same mind, and in the same
" judgment *." By this mutual love of order and peace, by this social affection, and general good conduct, you will distinguish

* 1 Cor. i. 10.

yourselves from men of unchristian principles, and will shew, that all your works, and all your views, are directed to the glory of God, the improvement of your nature, and the happiness of society.

Such, then, is a brief view,—and such as seemed more peculiarly applicable on this occasion,—of the nature, the tendency, and the spirit, of the Gospel of Christ. Much more might be added, to display the sublimity of its doctrines, and the purity of its laws. And, in every view in which it can be considered, it must appear so admirably adapted to our nature and infirmities, so congenial to the human mind, and so conducive to our happiness, that we cannot, if we attend to its peculiar excellence and evidences, but be convinced of its Divine origin, and be deeply impressed with gratitude to the Author of such a merciful dispensation.

And now, my brethren, on a review of all that has been said,—Consider what effect this religion has on your temper and conduct. It is by attention to these great duties and principles,

ciples, amidst the various occupations of active and laborious life, that you shew your "conversation" to be "such as becometh the "Gospel of Christ." Professing yourselves, then, to be Christians, have your thoughts, your words, and your actions, been regulated by Christianity? Owning yourselves candidates for another and higher state of existence, have your religious principles had an habitual influence on your hearts and lives? Have they led you, in every condition of life, to act conscientiously, and to avoid those vices, to which, from your situation, and natural temper, you were peculiarly exposed? Can you say, that you have revered and loved the God who made you, and the Saviour who redeemed you; that you have cherished benevolent affections towards all mankind without exception; and "kept yourselves unspotted "from the world?" Have you considered the important purpose for which you were created, and endeavoured to improve your moral nature? Conscious, as all of us must be, of numberless errors and imperfections, have your hopes of future happiness been founded on that mercy, which is most eminently displayed

played in the Gospel dispensation? Have you prayed earnestly, that the blessed influence of Divine Grace may enlighten your understandings, and enable you to improve in piety, in benevolence, in humility, and in all the other graces of the Christian character? Have you shewn your parental affection, by guarding your children against vicious habits, and by using your best endeavours to have them instructed in the duties of the Christian religion? Have you frequently reflected, that we are now in a state of probation for eternity; that God will make a distinction between the righteous and the wicked; and that the future destination of all good men will be—" to glory, honour, and immor-" tality?" And, in fine, amidst all the trials and afflictions of the world, have you been resigned to the dispensations of Providence, thankful that you are capable of moral improvement, and that " every event will," ultimately, " work together for your good?"

What answers some of *you* can give to enquiries of this sort, God and your own consciences know best. But, alas! we can too easily judge of many by their neglect of devotion, and of moral duties. When we consider the Gospel, as it is delineated in the New Testament, and compare it with the lives of many, who call themselves Christians, we are struck with the amazing contrast, and can hardly perceive any resemblance between them. The pleasures and the riches of the world on the one hand, and its business and anxieties on the other, often prevent men from paying that attention to the doctrines and precepts of our holy religion, which its infinite importance deserves.

In opposition to this conduct, let me remind you, that you are immortal beings. Six days you are allowed and enjoined to labour, and to procure an honest subsistence for yourselves and families. But the seventh day is the Sabbath of the Lord your God; he hath appropriated it to religious purposes, and has forbidden us to spend it in worldly pursuits. You should, therefore, come regularly to the House of God for the exercise of devotion, and attend, with unbiassed minds, to the religious instruction delivered from this place. All should then be engaged in the public

lic worship of Almighty God; all should be employed in imploring his mercy and protection. Trifling excuses should never be permitted to interfere with the important duty of social piety; and, if you are occasionally prevented from coming to church, you should be the more anxious to give your attendance at other times. By this means you will still maintain a sense of religion on your minds, and be sensible of the wise purposes, for which the Sabbath was instituted.

The wisdom and goodness of God, in setting apart one day in seven for our improvement in religion, can never be sufficiently admired. Without this divine institution, the bulk of mankind would continue in gross ignorance of every moral and religious principle; and, probably, would enjoy little or no interruption from the business and toils of life. How careful, then, should you all be, to avoid every encroachment on its proper and sacred employments! The Christian Sabbath tends to polish the manners, to promote the benevolence, and to improve the virtue and piety of mankind; and, by a cessation from labour and the ordinary occupations of life, it

gives

gives ease and relief, even to the brute-creation. Assisted by that sense of religion, which you acquire in the House of God, if, in the hour of temptation, you should deviate from the path of duty, there is reason to hope that a principle of piety and goodness may restrain you, and you may be enabled, through Divine Grace, to act with propriety for the time to come. But, when once men withdraw their attendance entirely from church, when they neglect the ordinances of Christianity, and despise the most solemn call to public devotion, the impressions of religion will wear off by degrees; and, among those who have hardly any other opportunity of knowing their duty to God and man, be assured, there is every reason to dread that, at last, they may become abandoned to profligacy and vice, and may commit the most atrocious crimes. Unhappy men! Let them remember the awful words of Scripture: "They that are far from God shall perish; but it is good for us to draw near to God." —I beseech you, therefore, to be regular in the duties of public worship, and come hither, every Lord's-day, with minds elevated with de-

devotion, and open to inftruction. You will find, that the pure and heavenly principles, which are here inculcated, afford the beft and moft foothing confolation to the human mind, amidft the numberlefs calamities to which we are expofed.

Public worfhip, then, is a part, a neceffary and indifpenfable part, of the duties of the Sunday, whatever may be your ftation in life. This is not all: the duties of public worfhip occupy only a fmall portion of that facred day. You fhould, therefore, fpend the remainder of it confiftently with your Chriftian views and profeffion. " Acquaint " yourfelves with God, and be at peace *." At a diftance from the tumult of the world, " Regard the works of the Lord, and con" fider the operation of his hands †." In your walks, in your converfation with your friends, in your retirement and devotions, by reading religious books, and efpecially the Bible, that bleffed fource of divine truth and confolation;—by all thefe means of reflexion and improvement, you may contemplate the

* Job, xxii. 21. † Ifaiah, v. 12.

stupendous works of Creation, of Providence, and of Redemption. The heavens, the earth, and the majestic river that flows by us, do all display their magnificent beauties to the poor as well as the rich, and should excite in the heart sentiments of piety; and, even while you are employed on other days in the business and duties imposed on you by your station, you may, from the wonderful œconomy of Nature, exhibited in the vicissitudes of the seasons, and in the several productions of the year, raise your thoughts to the Almighty Creator and Governor of the universe;—and thereby derive instruction and consolation to the mind. " The Sabbath was made for man"—to improve those faculties which are the chief ornament of his nature; to give him time and opportunity to call off his attention and attachment from the concerns of this short and precarious state of existence; and to direct his views to that final " rest, " which remaineth for the people of God*" to those " new heavens, and that new " earth, wherein dwelleth righteousness †."

* Heb. iv. 9.   † 2 Peter, iii. 13.

Be perfuaded, then, on every Lord's-day, to fufpend your cares and your bufinefs about this life, and to devote it to the momentous concerns of religion, and of *another* life. And in the time of profperity, and under all our infirmities and afflictions, let us confole ourfelves with the expectation, that, when we fhall no longer unite in prayer and praifes to the great Author of our being here on earth, where our beft fervices are attended with many imperfections,—if we be actuated in our conduct and " converfation" by the principles and duties of the Gofpel,—we fhall at laft be admitted, through the goodnefs of God, and the merits of our Redeemer, into that *heavenly* Society, where our faculties will be improved, and harmony and order will for ever prevail; and fhall unite with angels and archangels, and the fpirits of juft men made perfect, in a far more exalted and an eternal Hallelujah of praife. Amen.

ON THE STATE OF THE POOR,
AND
ON THE MEANS OF IMPROVING IT.

IT is the duty of every member of the community, to use his utmost exertions to promote the happiness of individuals and the prosperity of the state. Whether the condition of the labouring poor be better than at any former period, I will not take upon me to decide; but, certainly, it is not such as could be wished, on the principles, either of humanity, or of sound policy. It will still admit of considerable improvement, and be capable of receiving great alleviation, under the many trials and difficulties, which, in the common and necessary course of human life, do, and indeed must, press upon the lower orders of society, as well as upon every other. Different causes, no doubt, contribute to their distress, and to the prevalence of ignorance and vice among them; and various methods of improving their condition, and of reforming their morals, may be suggested. Of these causes and remedies,

I will

I will briefly ſtate ſome, which are very obvious, and deſerve to be conſidered with minute attention*.

I. One cauſe of diſtreſs among the poor is generally attributed to the advanced price of the neceſſaries of life. The fact, however, of the reward of agricultural labour not having riſen in proportion to the price of proviſions, is partially, but not generally, true †. And, it ſhould be obſerved, that the burden of poor-rates, and of other parochial and public taxes, has been very heavily increaſed upon every other claſs of ſociety.—It may, alſo, be proper to remark the impolicy of regulating the price of labour. It

---

* It would be too arduous a taſk for the Author, and would far exceed the limits of his plan, either to trace, through their various bearings and dependencies, all the cauſes which have combined to depreſs the intellects, and add to the miſeries, of the inferior claſſes of ſociety; or to enumerate all the plans which have been propoſed for their melioration and relief. But, amidſt a variety of uſeful publications on this ſubject, the political enquirer will derive much important information from Davies "On the Caſe of Labourers in Huſbandry;" from Ruggles's "Hiſtory of the Poor;" from M'Farlan's "Enquiries concerning the Poor;" and, particularly, from Sir Frederic Eden's very laborious and valuable work, "On the State of the Poor."

† See Sir Frederic Eden, *paſſim*; and Dr. Adam Smith's celebrated treatiſe "On the Wealth of Nations."

seems, indeed, to be impoffible, that any legiflative regulation on this fubject could ever be eftablifhed; and, were it practicable, it would not be ufeful; it would fupprefs a fpirit of emulation, and might produce greater mifchief, and more fenfible inconveniencies, than thofe which it was intended to remove.

II. Another great caufe of poverty, among many in the inferior ftations of life, is their idlenefs, their difinclination to labour and honeft induftry. Every means, therefore, fhould be ufed to reprefs this growing fpirit of lazinefs and improvidence, and to counteract their baneful effects in fociety. This can only be done, by furnifhing employment for the idle, and for thofe who are difpofed to work; by training them up to habits of induftry; and by fhewing them, that thereby, inftead of being a difgrace and nuifance to the ftate, the loweft peafant may become virtuous, ufeful, and refpectable.

To effect this important purpofe, the principal objects that claim public attention are the improvement of agriculture, manufactures, and commerce. Of thefe, agriculture, the induftry of the country, and the great fource of human provifion and of national profperity, deferves the *firft* place on feveral accounts: it is a moft healthy

healthy employment; it encourages marriage and population; it leads to plenty, and cheapness of provisions; it increases public and private wealth: and those who are employed in it are observed to be, in general, more peaceable, as well as more industrious members of society, and are less addicted to drunkenness and immorality, to turbulence and faction, than those who are engaged in sedentary occupations. Near great towns, where land has already attained a high state of cultivation, the importance of agricultural improvements will not be so striking; but, as a general object in the system of political œconomy, it merits the utmost attention.

To meliorate the condition of the industrious poor, by facilitating the means of their employment and subsistence, it will, perhaps, be necessary, in some cases, to supply them occasionally with proper materials at their own houses*, according to their age, their strength, and their capaci-

---

* It is a fact, that the poor are maintained much more comfortably, and at much less expence, at their own homes, than in workhouses, or houses of industry: their children, also, make hardier and better labourers. And many instances might be adduced, of the importance of providing constant employment for women and girls in knitting and spinning, &c. But the low rate of female labour is a great source of poverty, and tends to produce idleness.

ties; and to give suitable instructions and encouragement to those who are inclined to support themselves by their labour. And it may here be remarked, that, if the poor were thus profitably and constantly employed, they would be almost always able to maintain themselves and their families, their honest exertions seldom failing to supply their expences.—Were this principle, the fruit of active industry, universally diffused, mankind would see its great influence and importance, in the cultivation and improvement of those arts and sciences which tend to the convenience, the ornament, and the happiness of social life.

III. The poor-laws were humanely intended to relieve the distresses of the lower ranks of people; but experience has shewn, that they are extremely defective, both in their spirit, and in their execution. They ought, therefore, to be carefully and cautiously revised, and rendered as perfect as the combined wisdom of the legislature can devise: what is useful should be retained; and what has proved impolitic, or oppressive, should be modified, or repealed. In any alteration of these laws, care should be taken, that they promote virtue in general, and particularly temperance and frugality; and that they guard against vice, and especially drunkenness and extravagance: this regularity of conduct will be highly beneficial

beneficial to the lower ranks themfelves, and it will tend to reduce the exceffive amount of the poor's rates.

IV. Other caufes of general diftrefs among the poor, are their want of domeftic œconomy, their incommodious habitations, and their being bigoted to particular kinds of diet, and of drefs. It is to be lamented, that they pay too little attention to a judicious choice of wholefome and nutritious vegetables for diet: and hence, whenever there happens to be a failure of that particular crop of grain which conftitutes their principal food, their diftrefs furpaffes all defcription. Now, it would tend to alleviate their hardfhips, if they made their earnings more productive, by good management, by felecting cheap and palatable articles of diet, and by preparing different kinds of favoury foups *.

The poor are often blamed for their attachment to wheaten bread, and their fondnefs for tea. It is faid, and not without reafon, that, by drinking tea, inftead of home-brewed beer, their bodies

* See Count Rumford's interefting "Experimental Effays" for improving the condition and domeftic œconomy of the labouring poor.

On the means of diminifhing the confumption of *fuel*, which is fo effential a neceffary of life, and fo important an article to the lower claffes, his remarks claim particular attention.

become enervated, and their health is impaired. It ought, however, to be obſerved in their behalf, how natural it is for thoſe, who enjoy ſo few comforts in life, and are expoſed to ſo many difficulties, to endeavour to procure the beſt bread; eſpecially as they are ſeldom able to purchaſe meat. The high price of malt prevents them from brewing their own beer, as they did formerly; and this is a hardſhip, which drives many of them to the public houſe.

It would contribute much to their comfort, and to the preſervation of their health, if the agricultural poor had ſmall gardens, in which they could raiſe beans, peaſe, potatoes, greens, turnips, and other culinary vegetables; and if lords of manors, and men of affluence, would accommodate their labourers and dependents with neat and commodious cottages, at moderate rents. Many important advantages would reſult from this ſcheme, if generally adopted throughout the kingdom; and therefore it cannot be too ſtrongly recommended to the conſideration of the higher claſſes of ſociety. It muſt be allowed, that it would be the means of augmenting the quantity, and thereby reducing the price of pork, poultry, and fruit. Beſides, by increaſing the ſize of a poor man's garden, you add greatly to his comfort and enjoyment; and as, in ſome pariſhes, at a diſtance from populous towns, there is, uſually, waſte and unproductive

unproductive land contiguous to the cottages of the peasants, let a small portion of this land be allotted to the industrious labourer, and he will devote his evenings to its cultivation. As an encouragement to industry, and a reward for their services to the state, those who have brought up the most numerous families of children, without parochial aid, might have as much of the waste land appropriated to them as, when cultivated, would enable them to keep a cow.

The proprietors of land have it much in their power to alleviate the condition of poor farmers and day-labourers; and, by directing and assisting their industry, to render themselves and their dependents happy and useful to each other.

To a feeling mind, it is distressing to see the miserable cottages of many of the agricultural poor, and to think of the rents they pay for them. Now, if what is here suggested, were carried into general practice, it would be attended with the most beneficial effects: their houses would be more commodious; their mode of living would be more improved; their constitutions would be invigorated; their manners would be rendered more gentle and humane; and sentiments of mutual good-will would be excited among the different ranks of society. To which we may add, that, with these domestic comforts and improvements, the poor would not be so apt to debase

their

their moral faculties by vicious habits, but would acquire a higher fenfe of character, and would be gradually brought to a more fober and orderly way of life.—This leads me to obferve that,

V. The great number of public-houfes proves moſt pernicious to the health, the œconomy, and the morals of the poor, and may be reckoned one of the chief fources of their mifery. Nor need this be wondered at, when we confider, that the moſt nefarious practices are either planned or perpetrated in them. To thefe houfes you may trace almoſt every vice which becomes a difgrace and nuifance to fociety. For the poor, who are not burdened with very large families, only require fobriety and common induſtry to live comfortably; but, when thefe virtues are wanting, and they once acquire the ruinous habit of frequenting public houfes, which are often fchools of idlenefs and vice, they meet with profligate companions, who, by degrees, extinguifh every virtuous and honeft principle, and render them at laſt totally depraved.

In a populous city, the baneful effects of public houfes, though they be of the moſt ferious nature, are not always fo vifible to a common obferver, as in a country village. But it is impoſſible to defcribe, or even to imagine, how the morals of the lower claſſes of fociety are corrupted, how induſtry is checked, how agriculture and manufactures are retarded, and how many virtuous wives and innocent children are neglected and abandoned, in consequence of the enticements, which are every-where held forth to labourers, to spend their earnings, and drink intoxicating liquors at the ale-house.

An obvious and important method of giving an effectual check to this alarming evil would be, to diminish the number of public-houses, and to see that they be well regulated, and kept by men of decent manners, as well as of some property and responsibility. For this purpose, magistrates should refuse to license houses where they are not absolutely wanted, and where good order and regularity are not enforced: they should also limit the number in each district. From such regulations as these, thus carried into execution, the temptations to impiety and licentiousness would be reduced, and the most salutary effects, on the industry and sobriety of the poor, would result.

VI. In enumerating the various causes of misery among the inferior classes of the community, it is with deep concern I must mention their moral depravity, and their extreme backwardness to receive instruction; consequently, their general ignorance, and, what is frequently the result of it, unconquerable dispositions to a life of idleness and diffipation. Many of them are fo debafed in their minds, fo profligate in their manners, and fo diffolute in their purfuits, that immediate means fhould be taken to reprefs their alarming depravity, and to adopt fuch means as may correct the morals, and improve the intellects of the people *. It is, therefore, earneftly recommended to the public, to eftablifh Parochial Schools for educating the children of the poor, and for training them up with particular attention to the duties of morality and religion.

Where Sunday-fchools are properly eftablifhed, and conftantly infpected, they will be extremely ufeful, in refcuing many from ignorance and vice, and in diffufing, more widely, the genuine principles of the Gofpel. But this is a partial advantage : in many parifhes there are no fuch inftitutions, and the poor are often unable to pay for the education of their children. Some more general plan is therefore wanted, by which all the moft indigent, the moft illiterate, and the moft wretched claffes of fociety, may be taught to read, and be inftructed in the doctrines and duties of Chriftianity. This, befides other unfpeakable advanta-

---

* Examples, however, of immoral conduct are not confined to the *lower* claffes of the people ; they pervade all ranks. The poor naturally adopt the fentiments, and imitate the manners of the rich ; and in nothing more than in profligacy and impiety.

ges, would prepare them for those public instructions from the pulpit which, for want of such previous culture, cannot be so well understood, or so deeply impressed on the mind. An institution of this sort, by which the rising generation might be taught reading, writing, and arithmetic, is a national object of the greatest magnitude. With the assistance of Sunday-schools, it would prevent many wrong habits in early life; and it would gradually and effectually remove that extreme ignorance which disgraces the lower orders of the community, and, no doubt, adds much to their immorality. Of such importance is the establishment of Parochial Schools, that, I am persuaded, the children in the inferior ranks cannot, by any other plan, be so effectually and so extensively trained up to the business and duties of human life.

Without entering into the particular manner of accomplishing this design*, it may be observed, that persons, properly qualified, should be appointed with adequate salaries, which might be paid by a parish rate; and their chief object should be, to teach children to read and write, to give them practical instructions, and to di-

---

* See Dr. Chapman's excellent treatise on Education, 5th edit. to which are subjoined some useful observations on the instruction necessary for the lower ranks of the people; on the appointment of parochial school-masters; and on the encouragement they ought to receive.

rect and superintend their conduct. There is no reason to be alarmed at the expence, as much larger sums are annually raised for less beneficial pupofes. In Scotland and Switzerland, which are poorer countries than this, Parochial Schools are established, and have been followed with the most general good effects. Part of the expences should be defrayed by the parish; and part of them by the parents. The terms for teaching to read, and for explaining the Church-Catechism, should be so moderate, that even a common labourer may afford the expence, of giving his children these most essential branches of education.

All young people require some recreation for the benefit of their health. This recreation should have in view the occupations for which they are probably designed. It is worthy, therefore, of remark, that the utmost attention should be paid to early industry. To this end, during the intervals of public instruction, their time should not be entirely wasted in unprofitable diversion. In the country, they might, according to their age and ability, be gradually inured to the business of agriculture; and in towns, to the easiest operations of manufactures.

By thus training the children of the poor to early habits of industry, piety, and morality, a perfect system of education would be produced; and they would, thereby, be qualified for the arduous

arduous duties of social and active life. By establishing proper salaries for parochial teachers, and by infusing into the young mind those virtuous and Christian principles which the institution of Sunday-schools has a tendency to promote, we shall have no longer occasion to complain of the idleness, the dishonesty, and the turbulence of the poor. With these means of instruction, and of reformation, applied to the mass of the people, they would, by degrees, be formed to useful labour, to a Christian temper, and to the practice of those momentous duties which we owe to God and man.

Thus a most important change would soon be effected in their *manners*, and in their *morals*. Thus, a sense of religion, and all the good effects of it, would insensibly arise, and be gradually increased among the poor. They would begin to raise their drooping spirits, and to acquire more animating views of Providence, of religious and moral obligation, and of the great end for which they were sent into the world. Ignorance, immorality, and superstition, would give way to knowledge, virtue, and truth; and mankind would be convinced, that religion does not consist merely in external forms and ceremonies, but—in self-government, in benignity, in "worshipping God in spirit and in truth"—and in discharging

charging with fidelity the duties of their refpective ftations.

With regard to the inftruction of the female fex, I fhall only remark, that, in every civilized country, even the loweft claffes fhould not only be taught to fpin, to knit, and to few, but alfo to read the Bible, and to underftand the important truths of Chriftianity. The utmoft pains fhould be taken, to fhew them that virtue and vice are effentially different; to infpire them, in early life, with the love of the one, and to guard them againft the feductions of the other; to warn them of the dangers of bad habits, and of bad company; to point out to them the happinefs which naturally attends innocence, modefty, and good conduct, and the mifery which inevitably follows impropriety of behaviour, profligacy of manners, and lofs of reputation. Young women, on their entrance into life, cannot be too much guarded againft feduction; nor can their minds be too ftrongly fortified, by religious principles, againft thofe enfnaring temptations, to which, at that early period, they are peculiarly expofed; for, unlefs virtuous and religious habits are then formed, they are feldom acquired afterwards; and it is obvious, that a train of the moft grievous and complicated evils muft enfue, when once a woman lofes her virtue and chaftity, and debafes her character by diffolute manners, and

a cria criminal life. Hence, as the crime of seduction produces the most serious mischief in society, it deserves a very severe punishment.

My subject has only led me to offer some hints concerning the nature and degree of instruction necessary for those who are probably destined by Providence to fill the lowest ranks of life, and must labour for their daily subsistence. But, as it refers to an object of great and general importance, I must be permitted to observe further, that, in the prevailing system of modern education, there is an essential defect: the attention of the teacher is not sufficiently directed to the culture and improvement of the mind; the morals of the children are often neglected; and the primary objects of education,—the inculcating of virtuous and religious principles, and the enforcing of them by proper discipline,—generally occupy little attention, both in public and in private schools. But, high as our esteem should be for classical, scientific, and philosophical pursuits, and for those ornamental acquirements which contribute to the innocent amusement of domestic life; yet the chief solicitude of every parent, who believes in a future state, should be, to preserve the innocence, to cultivate the understanding, and to govern the passions, of his children. And, indeed, we may look in vain for a reformation of manners in society, while religious

ligious impreffions, and moral habits, in educating our youth of both fexes, are fo much neglected.

I have dwelt thus long on this fubject, from a conviction, that the right education of youth would be productive of the moft beneficial confequences, that it would be the moft effectual means of promoting the beft and moft important interefts of mankind; and that the poorer claffes of fociety are entitled to the attention and affiftance of the more opulent.

VII. Another caufe of diftrefs among the poor, and the laft I fhall mention, is their general improvidence in the days of youth, and in the earlier part of life. To counteract this want of œconomy, and of prudence, which leads many of them to make little or no provifion for the various accidents and calamities to which human nature is continually expofed, and to infpire the lower orders with manly fentiments, no method appears fo well calculated as the general diffufion of *Friendly Societies*. To thefe beneficial inftitutions, then, I fhall now call the reader's ferious attention, and fhall evince, that, if properly encouraged, and duly regulated, very folid benefits, indeed, might be derived from their extenfion.

There is something in the very name peculiarly congenial to the benevolent and social nature of man, exciting his compassion for his fellow-creatures in the hour of sickness and distress, and leading him to sympathize with them under all their afflictions. Some plans, which have been devised for the maintenance of the poor, have a tendency to depress energy, and to promote idleness, and inattention to futurity; but it is to the credit of these Friendly Societies, that they have industry, foresight, and philanthropy, for their basis.

A poor man, by paying three-pence, or fourpence *per* week, while he is young and in health, is entitled to relief in the time of sickness, and under the infirmities of old age, and secures a decent provision, which renders him independent. By this means, he is exempt from those anxious and desponding moments, which reflections on the uncertainty of health, and the dread of accidents and want, might otherwise occasion. The payments are so trifling, that he does not feel himself deprived by them of any domestic comfort; and they prove to be the happy means of making him more industrious, more prudent, and more virtuous.—Let us here appeal to a few facts, which are of a very interesting nature, and well merit an ample discussion.

There are two Friendly Societies at Sunbury, consisting of about 120 members. They are both

both in a flourishing condition, and have some property in the funds; a circumstance which tends to attach them to the established government. One of them was instituted in December 1773, and has now (October 1797) in the 4 *per cent. Consols.* £.666 11*s.* 5*d.*; and the other, instituted in 1787, has, in the 3 *per cent. Consols,* £.275. It is unnecessary for me to mention all the rules that are established by these Friendly Societies; but, for the information of those who are unacquainted with the nature and design of such useful institutions, I will here state some of the most important.

The rules of the societies are nearly the same. In the oldest club, no one is admitted a member who is not in good health, and (formerly) between 18 and 40 years of age: now it is limited from 18 to 30 years. The terms of admission were originally 2*s.* 6*d.* but are since raised to 10*s.* 6*d.* Every member, who is not incapacitated by illness or old age, pays one shilling and threepence *per* month; the threepence for beer, and the shilling for the relief of those who shall be sick, lame, or blind. But he can derive no benefit from the fund till he hath subscribed to it two years; after which, during illness and inability to work, he receives seven shillings *per* week. On the death of a free member, seven pounds are allowed to defray the expences of his funeral, and for the benefit of his widow, or nearest relation:

on thefe occafions, each member pays a fhilling for the farther fupport of the fociety. And, on the death of a free member's wife, two pounds are allowed towards the funeral expences.

To guard againſt frauds and idleneſs, it is found neceſſary, that the weekly allowance to ſick members fhould be rather leſs than their ufual earnings. Time, and the public attention, it may be hoped, will correct many errors, and lead to much improvement, in the regulation of Friendly Societies. It is to be regretted, that the public have hitherto obtained ſo little information on this interefting fubject. By comparing various particulars, which old eftablifhed clubs could furnifh, it might be calculated, with greater precifion, whether the allowance be in proportion to the contributions, or where any defect has originated. Neither of the focieties at Sunbury has been inftituted fo long, as to enable me to give all the information which could be wifhed; I flatter myfelf, however, that the following ftatement, from the oldeft club, will not be unacceptable to the reader, as it will help to eftablifh fome ufeful documents, and may encourage the gentry, tradefmen, and farmers, in other parifhes, to become honorary members of fuch valuable inftitutions. It is, in fact, their wifeft policy, and that for more cogent reafons than need be mentioned.

An

An Abstract of the Subscriptions, and Disbursements, in the Friendly Society held at the White-Horse, Sunbury, from December 1773 to October 1797.

Years.	No. of members.	Deaths of members.	Deaths of members wives.	Subscriptions, fines, interest, &c.			Subscriptions of honorary members.			Payments to sick; and at funerals, &c.			Savings.			State of the fund.		
				£.	s.	d.	£.	s.	d.	£.	s.	d.	£.	s.	d.	£.	s.	d.
1774	48	—	—	28	15	8	—	—	—	*{8	3	9½	20	11	10½	20	11	10½
1775	51	—	—	42	19	3	—	—	—	{8	15	4	34	3	11	54	15	9½
1776	59	—	1	39	3	1	—	—	—	6	1	9	33	1	4	87	17	1½
1777	60	—	1	38	12	1½	—	—	—	21	2	8	17	9	5½	105	6	7
1778	60	—	—	40	12	6	1	1	0	15	16	6	25	17	0	131	3	7
1779	61	—	—	46	4	9	3	3	0	12	10	11	36	16	10	168	0	5
1780	61	—	1	41	4	9	1	1	0	20	3	9	22	2	0	190	2	5
1781	61	1	—	46	7	6	†10	10	0	30	7	10	26	10	1	216	12	6
1782	61	—	—	48	0	11½	3	3	0	21	8	1	29	15	10½	246	8	4½
1783	61	—	—	48	4	7	2	2	0	25	13	4	24	13	3	271	1	7½
1784	61	—	1	61	5	0	3	3	0	23	5	8	41	2	4	312	3	11½
1785	61	—	1	63	8	7	2	2	0	65	2	8	0	7	11	312	11	10½
1786	61	—	2	53	5	0	2	2	0	24	16	3	30	10	9	343	2	7½
1787	61	—	2	61	12	6	2	2	0	38	10	5	25	4	1	368	6	8½
1788	61	2	2	63	7	7½	3	3	0	44	11	7½	21	19	0½	390	5	9
1789	61	—	—	56	5	5	3	3	0	28	11	9	30	15	8	421	2	5
1790	61	—	—	58	19	10	3	3	0	27	12	9	34	10	1	455	12	6
1791	61	1	—	52	5	9	5	5	0	52	4	5	5	6	4	460	18	10
1792	61	2	1	60	11	5	4	4	0	62	4	10	2	10	7	463	9	5
1793	60	—	1	59	14	11	4	4	0	62	9	0	1	9	11	464	19	4
1794	59	—	1	69	16	5	4	4	0	38	4	8	35	15	9	500	15	1
1795	58	1	—	59	11	3	3	13	6	35	19	6½	27	5	2½	528	0	3½
1796	57	1	—	60	17	3	7	7	0	43	8	11½	24	15	5½	552	15	9
1797	57	—	3	40	11	10	8	8	0	26	10	6	14	1	4½	‡566	17	1
							£.77	3	6									

* No allowance to sick members the first and second year; these sums were for articles, books, box, clerk, &c.
† Lord Hawke left a legacy of five guineas.
‡ This has purchased, at different times, £.666. 11s. 5d. stock in the four per Cents.

From this statement it appears, that our subscriptions, as honorary members, have amounted to £.77 3s. 6d., and, though the funds of the society are not yet stationary, that the expences of supporting sick members have, of late, increased much more rapidly than at first. The reason is obvious: some of the members are beginning to decline into the vale of life, and consequently require more frequent relief than they did when they were in the vigour of manhood. It is, therefore, probable, that, twenty or thirty years hence, the fund will be lower than at present; though, there is reason to hope that, with prudent management, it is founded on principles which will secure its permanence and success*.

To shew the utility of Friendly Societies in reducing the poor's rates, it will be only necessary to observe, that, by taking an average of the six years, previous to their institution at Sunbury in 1773, when provisions were much cheaper than at present, the poor-rates were 2s. 9d. in the pound; sometimes they were as high as 3s. 6d. But, as the societies began to flourish, a gradual reduction has taken place; and, by their com-

---

* As the other society has only been instituted a few years, it seems unnecessary to give an abstract of the state of its funds; it consists almost entirely of young members, and meets with similar encouragement from honorary subscribers.

bined

bined effects, the poor-rates have been as low as 1*s.* 6*d.*; and, during the fix years previous to 1796, never higher than 1*s.* 9*d.* Now, many of the members are fo indigent, that, if they happen to be ill for a fhort time, and are thereby rendered incapable of following their bufinefs, they muft inevitably apply for *parochial* relief, had they not recourfe to a fund, which their own induftry, their œconomy, and their honeft pride, have contributed to raife.

That Friendly Societies, then, tend confiderably to the relief and fupport of the poor is obvious; and their eftablifhment is no lefs ufeful to the public than beneficial to the members who compofe them. When the morals of the lower ranks of fociety are more reformed, and their children are better inftructed, a greater degree of induftry and temperance will arife among them, and they will feel more fenfibly the degradation of trufting to the fupport of parifh-relief. It feems that thefe inftitutions have already had fomething of this effect at Sunbury, and may partly account for the rates being fo moderate.

In favour of poor-rates and work-houfes it may be alledged, that they are ufeful, as they have afforded relief and an afylum to orphans, to the aged, to the helplefs, and to the difabled,—to thofe who, otherwife, might poffibly have perifhed through want, or might have been reduced to the utmost distress: that they oblige the rich, the inconsiderate, and the avaricious, as well as the liberal and the humane, to contribute according to their abilities, or to the rent of the houses and grounds they occupy; and, though abused, as most institutions are, in proportion to their goodness, that they create one most important and essential distinction between the comforts and security of the lower orders here, and in every other country under Heaven.

But, on the other hand, it ought to be admitted, that, in a political view, they are extremely detrimental: they fall very heavy on the middling, and most productive, classes of society; they debase the minds of the lowest, and relax the exertions of honest industry, rendering men less provident, and less attached to the interest and welfare of their families. As the society of workhouses is composed of the worst characters and tempers, it is not to be wondered at, that it should frequently be disturbed by quarrels and contentions. To a peaceable and virtuous mind they always prove uncomfortable situations.

Let it be next considered, that the children brought up in them are seldom so healthy, or become such good servants, as the children of cottagers. They have given rise to the Law of Settlements, which is as impolitic as it is oppressive,

five, and has proved a conſtant ſource of litigation between pariſhes, as well as a great diſcouragement to induſtry. In this reſpect, they are found to be prejudicial to the comfort of the poor, and to the intereſts of ſociety. And, after all, it may even be doubted whether they leſſen the number of perſons claiming relief.

Objections, alſo, of a *moral* nature, may be juſtly urged againſt them, as they tend to diminiſh private charity, and to make men inattentive to the afflictions of others. Beſides, workhouſes are generally prejudicial to the health, the comfort, and the morals of the poor. They often weaken the principles of natural affection; they lead the lower ranks to uſe little or no exertions to preſerve their poor relations from what ought to be conſidered as a reproach; and they are ſo little attended to, that they too frequently become ſcenes of idleneſs, and even of vice. They are ſupported at an enormous expence, and produce—miſery and diſcontent.

Though the ſums collected at celebrating the Sacrament of the Lord's Supper are generally inconſiderable, yet, when they are diſtributed in a judicious manner, by the reſident miniſter, among the aged and impotent poor, during ſickneſs, and as their neceſſities may require, perhaps greater benefits are derived from theſe ſmall contributions, and more important and timely relief is administered, than even by the immense sums annually expended for the support of the parish workhouse.

To mention but one remark more—Were all Christians actuated by the benevolent principles of their religion, and did all regularly attend the public worship of God, the mode of providing for the poor, recommended by St. Paul*, and still practised in Holland, and in Scotland, with the happiest effects,—by making weekly collections in the churches, and by private donations,—is preferable to any other that could be devised. But, unfortunately,—many of the rich and the great, seldom or never frequent any place of religious worship: and many of them are immersed in fashionable dissipation, and reside at a distance from their estates †.

But,

---

* 1 Corin. xvi. 1, 2.

† This disadvantage, under which rural industry labours, might be remedied, by an application from the minister and church-wardens in England, as is usual from the minister and elders in Scotland, to the proprietors of houses and lands in the parish, requesting an occasional donation, suited to the necessities of the poor. This would be attended with no expence, and, being considered as a voluntary act, would be chearfully complied with, in preference to a poor-tax, imposed by law, and levied at considerable trouble and expence. On such applications, the proprietors of estates, &c. might

But, without entering farther into difquifitions, to which thefe remarks might lead, I fhall only obferve, that the poor muft become fober, orderly, and virtuous, and muft ultimately depend on their own exertions and good management, before any confiderable improvement can be made in their condition. While a man is able, by his diligence and œconomy, to earn a comfortable maintenance for himfelf and family, he fhould not degrade himfelf, by indolence or vice, to the ftate of a mendicant, and live on the induftry of others. But, when he has been frugal and diligent from his early youth, when once difeafe, infirmities, or age, have rendered him incapable of labour, then, and not till then, ought he to expect fupport. On thefe principles, which cannot be controverted, Friendly Societies deferve particular encouragement, as they call forth the beft exertions of every individual, and are the chief means of *preventing* poverty.

Both thefe focieties, as hath been already obferved, are compofed of mechanics, poor tradefmen,

---

might meet and tax themfelves, in proportion to their valued rents, as is done in many parifhes of Scotland; one half of the aflefiment to be paid by the proprietors, and the other half by the tenants.

and

and labourers in hufbandry. Now, let it be here remembered, as a fact of peculiar importance to the public, and as fubftantiating a moft valuable political truth, that although many of the members are burdened with numerous families, though they refide in one of the moft expenfive villages in the kingdom, and have no higher wages than others to fupport themfelves, though, like other focieties, they be compofed of a mixture of good and bad members, though they be liable to, and meet with, the fame calamities and accidents which befal others, and, under God, have only their own induftry and forefight to depend upon; yet, with all thefe difficulties to encounter, and while the expences of providing for the poor have been almoft doubled during the laft twenty years,—partly owing to the profligacy and impofitions of the poor, and partly to the inattention and mifmanagement of overfeers; notwithftanding thefe difadvantages, all the members of thefe focieties have fupported themfelves and families, and (except in one inftance of uncommon diftrefs*), have never received, fince their inftitution, the leaft affiftance from the parifh of Sunbury,

* The poor family here alluded to had an allowance of three fhillings a week for a few weeks!

The inference then, from all this, is as clear as it is important. By Friendly Societies, and by their beneficial operation, the neceffity of poor's rates might, in time, be in a great meafure, fuperfeded. The idle, the improvident, and the vicious, have been too apt to depend on the parochial fund; but it has proved a dangerous refource; always involving the thoughtlefs object that relies on it in the deepeft depravity and wretchednefs. Experience has clearly evinced, that poor's rates have not anfwered the benevolent purpofes for which they were defigned; and I am convinced, were they at firft limited in every parifh, then gradually diminifhed, and at laft entirely abolifhed, the lower orders of men would live much more comfortably, and much more virtuoufly, than they do at prefent.

At the fame time, it is farther obferved, that, where workhoufes have been long eftablifhed, they ought not to be given up at once, for fear of producing great diforder, and many inconveniences. All that can be expected is, that their abufes may be removed in fuch a gradual manner, as to create no difturbances; and that overfeers be partly guided, for fome time at leaft, by the cuftom of the parifh, till a better method of providing for the poor be adopted, till charity be brought back to its proper channel, voluntary contributions.

With respect to the mode of providing for the poor, it has already been affirmed, that, instead of workhouses, they might be supported much more comfortably, and at a much cheaper rate, at their own homes, by weekly or monthly allowances. But, in settling this allowance, a considerable distinction should be made, according to the character and circumstances of those who apply for parochial aid.—In the fluctuating state of commerce and manufactures, some will require occasional relief; and, when they are disabled from working by sickness or accident, a provision should be made for them until they are restored to health. But it will be generally found, that most of the poor are able to earn something for their support; so that a very small sum, added to their own industry and sobriety, would be sufficient to supply the deficiency of their labour.

Those who have been notoriously slothful and profligate might wear a badge, and receive an allowance, merely sufficient to support them with the meanest provisions; while the aged and disabled, who are of good characters, and have been in better circumstances, should have a more comfortable subsistence. And the utmost attention must be paid by the overseers of the poor, that the allowance to any on the pension-list be diminished, or entirely withdrawn, as soon as a change of circumstances will admit.

To promote order, and to reprefs idlenefs and vice, all vagrants and refractory perfons fhould be fent to the houfe of correction, and confined, for a longer or fhorter time, according to the nature and frequency of their offences. With proper attention, thefe houfes might be ufeful for reforming, as well as for punifhing, the idle and abandoned. Though humanity inclines us to pity the diftrefs, and to relieve the wants, of our fellow-creatures, yet the general interefts of fociety feem to require, that none, who are fupported by public charity, fhould enjoy the fame comforts of life as the induftrious labourer, or fhould receive fuch an ample allowance as to give encouragement to idlenefs.

As overfeers are appointed for one year only, they have hardly acquired a fufficient knowledge of the characters and ftate of the poor, when others, equally ignorant, fucceed them. To remedy this, they might be allowed to remain in office for a longer term, but fhould be refponfible for their management during their continuance in it. Or, rather, might not a committee be appointed by every parifh to meet at leaft once a month, and to fuperintend and tranfact all bufinefs relative to the poor? Thofe who are concerned in the management of the poor's funds, fhould be men of known integrity, vigilance, impartiality, and humanity. It fhould be their duty ty to enquire into the situation and characters, and even to visit the houses of those, who either receive, or are likely to solicit, public charity. By this means, a proper discrimination might be made between the idle and worthless, and those who are industrious and deserving objects of compassion. They could thereby judge what relief they may require, and how it may be bestowed with the greatest advantage. And, once every month, a minute enquiry should be made of the age, the infirmities, the number of children, the condition, and the *earnings*, of all the poor on the pension-list, before the allowance for the ensuing month be settled.

This would diminish the number of the poor, and the expence of supporting them. While the impositions of the clamorous and dissolute would thus be checked, the sober and industrious poor would be properly provided for. By making this distinction, we should feel the strongest inclination to give relief to the infirm, the diseased, and the helpless. Such persons have a right to our charity, either public or private. We are prompted by the dictates of our nature, and are enjoined by the precepts of our religion, to acts of beneficence. But, by a poor's rate, what was an amiable virtue is converted into a burdensome tax.

In other countries, no legal assessment is established

blished for the relief of the poor; the poor depend on the compassion of their fellow-creatures for their support. In this country then, so eminently distinguished for the number and variety of its charitable institutions, and while benevolence and humanity are, and we trust will continue to be, the characteristic of the British nation, it cannot be supposed, that the industrious, but unfortunate poor, meeting with any uncommon pressure of difficulties, would ever be forgotten or unpitied. On the contrary, private individuals would take the utmost pains to find out, and relieve, every deserving object of commiseration; their beneficence would be dispensed with prudence; and a spirit of real philanthropy, and of virtuous industry, would every where revive. The rich would then bestow their charity with pleasure, and the poor would receive it with gratitude.

That the poor may derive the greatest benefit from the liberality of the rich, it is to be observed, that some judgment must be used as to the time and mode of dispensing charity; and proper enquiry should be made for selecting the most worthy and necessitous objects. If a man's station, his avocations, or his health, preclude him from having a general knowledge of the state of the labouring poor in his neighbourhood, let him consult those who are well acquainted with their characters

racters and condition; and let him pay particular attention to their diftrefs in winter, in ficknefs, want of employment, and old age.

This remark is the more neceffary to be made, as charity, indifcriminately beftowed, encourages idlenefs and diffipation, which are principal caufes of the increafing number of the poor. The poor-laws hold out a certain provifion for their fupport, without making hardly any diftinction between thofe who have rendered themfelves poor by indolence or vice, and thofe who are reduced to a ftate of indigence by unavoidable misfortunes. And hence the moft flothful and criminal are well lodged, clothed, and fed, at the public expence; while the moft ufeful and deferving members of fociety fubfift on a more fcanty pittance, and only receive what they earn by hard labour.

Some have thought that all, who have not large families to fupport, fhould be compelled to fubfcribe to fome friendly or parochial club. The idea however of compulfion is revolting to the mind. Compulfion would impofe a fecond poor-tax, and that to be levied from a clafs of men who are leaft able to pay it. Parliament certainly meant to protect and encourage Friendly Societies by the act paffed in their behalf; yet it has excited fuch alarms among them *, that

---

* On this account, the focieties at Sunbury have declined to have their rules confirmed by the Magiftrates.

any farther attempts to regulate them might prove fatal to the inſtitution. At preſent, the members are actuated by a noble ſpirit of independence, as well as of induſtry and œconomy, which cannot be too highly commended; but, if recourſe were ever had to compulſive meaſures, it would ſtifle every ingenuous and liberal ſentiment, and render men mere machines.

Every thing ſhould be done by perſuaſion and example; and as the farmer is particularly intereſted in the maintenance of the poor, he has the ſtrongeſt motive to promote the eſtabliſhment of Friendly Societies by his advice, and to aſſiſt them by his contributions. Such arguments ſhould be uſed as are adapted to the temper, the habits, and condition of the lower claſſes of the community, and are likely to ſtimulate the latent principles of activity and induſtry within them; to warn them of the ſad degradation of applying for parochial relief, without abſolute neceſſity; to excite them, in their youth and health, to make a proper proviſion for ſickneſs or age; and thus to extricate themſelves from that debaſement of mind, that corruption of morals, and that inattention to future concerns, into which many of them are unhappily plunged.

The parochial clergy, aided by the higher and middle claſſes of life, might be extremely uſeful in bringing Friendly Societies into public notice, in explaining their nature, their importance, and their utility, and in thus promoting their general eftablifhment. To their ferious and candid confideration, then, thefe Friendly Societies, calculated, under proper regulations, to anfwer the moft beneficial ends to poor and rich, are earneftly recommended *.

Upon the whole : when we fee men fo ignorant and depreffed as the lower orders of fociety too frequently are, often indeed in confequence of their own imprudence, their idlenefs, their profligacy, and their crimes, it is lefs furprifing to find them carelefs and improvident about the future, negligent of the great and momentous concerns of religion, and unmindful of a higher and better ftate of exiftence. They are often exhorted to go to church, and to attend to the moft important fubjects that can occupy the mind of man. But, many of them alas! are dead to every religious impreffion, and alive to little, beyond fome tranfient purfuit of gain, or of trivial amufements; fo that, when we confider their poverty, and their ignorance,—the wretched ftate of their bodies, and of their minds,—a benevolent heart

---

* It is much to be wifhed, that the Legiflature, the Board of Agriculture, the Society for the encouragement of Arts, Manufactures, and Commerce, or the Society for bettering the condition of the poor, would offer premiums for the beft practical differtation on this important fubject.

will

will shed a tear over their misconduct, and will use the utmost efforts to correct their vices, to encourage their industry, to alleviate their afflictions, to improve their morals, and thereby to lead them progressively on to higher degrees of civilization, virtue, and happiness.

It is with this view, that these strictures, with the annexed rules, are submitted to the judgment of the public, in hopes they may be useful; and particularly among the author's parishioners, whose welfare he has always had much at heart. Some of them relate to plans of national improvement, and refer to subjects of general importance to society; and others, it is hoped, will prove beneficial to individuals, where parliamentary regulations are not requisite.

The author of these remarks, wishing them to be generally understood, has not attempted to recommend them by a high and elaborate style, or by very deep thought and research. But, if they have any tendency to guard the rich, on the one hand, against oppression, dissoluteness of manners, and a luxurious and thoughtless mode of living, and the poor, on the other, against idleness, intemperance, and discontent; if they have a tendency, also, to promote industry, œconomy, and foresight; to dispel ignorance, to enlighten and humanize the mind, and to excite men to the faithful discharge of the functions of their station, according to their various talents and situations; thus producing rectitude of principle, and a benevolent union between the higher and lower ranks of society; they may be of some moment in the present awful crisis; and whoever treats of these topics, in a manner worthy of their importance, will meet with candour and attention from the public. Nor is the author sanguine enough to expect, that these hints, however conducive to benevolence, civilization, and good government, will be adopted all at once. Mankind are in a state of progressive improvement in knowledge and virtue; but it is by gradual, and oftentimes by imperceptible means, that beneficial changes are effected.

Thus, by considering the external, and then the internal, condition of man, it appears, that he is commonly the chief author of his own sufferings; and that the greatest calamities he undergoes are principally owing to himself, and to his own misconduct in life. In some cases, however, we have seen, that his distress proceeds from causes which are adventitious; from events, which his prudence could not prevent; and from dispensations of Providence, which his wisdom could not controul. And, in a few instances, these causes may be so combined, as to leave it doubtful, whether he is most to be pitied, or to be blamed. But, whether the distresses of mankind arise arife from natural or from moral caufes, from the unavoidable calamities of life, or from the evil of fin, God has mercifully provided remedies by the confolations of religion. Chriftianity peculiarly claims our regard, as it accommodates itfelf, with great benignity, to our frailties and errors, and to the various inftances of worldly affliction, adminiftering confolation to us under our temporal or our fpiritual diftreffes. The difcoveries of Chriftianity are emphatically ftyled " glad tidings to the *poor*," to the indigent and illiterate, to thofe who are deftitute of worldly riches, or of religious knowledge. Our religion fhews us, that we are always under the protection of a wife and good Providence, and diffufes a fpirit of contentment, refignation, humanity, and piety, over all who fincerely embrace it. It has taught men to love each other, by inculcating this fublime and benevolent doctrine—That we are all children of the fame Heavenly Parent, all liable to the fame accidents, and all accountable for our conduct to the great Author of our being. It is peculiarly calculated to foothe the mind, when labouring under forrow and the impreffions of guilt, and enables us to bear with patience and fortitude whatever trials Providence may fee fit to appoint. To the penitent and fincere, whofe hearts are foftened and improved by affliction and a fenfe of duty; to the poor and the rich, who are actuated by the great principles of our religion; it gives the animating profpect of a bleffed immortality, of a happy ceffation from all moral diforders, and of a perpetual reft from the troubles and viciffitudes of human life.—But to return to the fubject of Friendly Societies.

Before I conclude, it may be proper to offer a few remarks on *Female* Benefit-clubs. All my obfervations confirm me in my opinion that, in tendernefs and benevolence, in fenfibility and attachment, in parental affection and folicitude, in delicacy of fentiment, and purity of conduct, in œconomy, and the conscientious difcharge of all the functions of a quiet, a virtuous, and a pious life; in all thefe important refpects, the female character is, in general, peculiarly amiable and praife-worthy; and it rarely happens, that a family falls into embarraffments through the mifconduct of the mother.

When a labourer is thus bleffed with a frugal, an induftrious, and intelligent wife, he fhews his attachment and good fenfe by leaving all domeftic concerns to her prudent and fuperior management. And he fhould be thankful to Providence, for beftowing " a help-mate for him," to alleviate the burden and forrows of life; to participate with him, in mutual intereft and endearment, in reciprocal duties, in conjugal affection and fidelity; to be a friend, and affociate in health and ficknefs,

nefs, in profperity and adverfity; and to cooperate with him, in infufing the principles of virtue and piety into the minds of their children.

The bufinefs of Female Societies is generally conducted by rules, in moft refpects, fimilar to thofe in clubs for men. A Female club, formed on the following payments, and allowances in cafes of illnefs, might be extremely ufeful among the poor, and would probably flourifh; efpecially under the patronage and infpection of any lady of diftinction. The age of admiffion to be between eighteen and forty; every fubfcriber, under twenty-five years of age, to pay 1*s.* of entrance-money; from twenty-five to thirty years of age, to pay 2*s.* and 6*d.*; and from thirty to forty, to pay 5*s.*, befides 6*d.* for the articles: to meet once a month, and each member to contribute 6*d.* to the fund.—After fubfcribing a year, to receive an allowance of 3*s.* a week, during the firft three month's illnefs; 2*s.* 6*d.* a week, during the next three month's illnefs; and 2*s.* a week afterwards, while a member is confined to her room, and is wholly difabled from any kind of work.—Every free member, on her lying-in, to receive 10*s.* 6*d.*; and each member to pay 2*d.* to the fund. On the death of a free member, 2*l.* to be allowed towards the funeral-expences, each member contributing 6*d.*: when the fund is, at any time, lefs than 50*l.*, every member to pay 6*d.* a quarter extra into the box.—Women's earnings are, in general, so small, that it will be found necessary, to make the monthly payments thus moderate; and, as they are more liable to sickness than men, their demands on the club must be proportionably lessened.

With respect to expences at their meetings, it may be remarked that, in some societies, 1d. or 2d. are paid by each individual: and sometimes it is spent in tea. But, when the business of Female Societies can be managed, without incurring any expence, and their meetings can be held at the house of any of the members, or when a private room can be hired for the purpose, it would be extremely desirable, as the most effectual means of silencing the envy, the malevolence, and the calumny of their adversaries.

In every female club, the following rule should be established and adhered to—" That, if any " single or unmarried woman should lead an idle, " profligate life, or be with child, while she be- " longs to the society, she shall be expelled." Such a regulation tends to promote chastity, and to discountenance immorality, and dissoluteness of manners.

Some Female Societies give no allowance to any member during the time of her pregnancy, and for a month after she is confined. I own, I do not entirely approve of the principles on which

which such a society seems to be instituted; but it gives me an opportunity of suggesting a method, by which poor married women may derive great comfort and relief, at a season too when they are exposed to considerable expence, and require peculiar assistance. I shall not, therefore, from motives of false delicacy, scruple to mention it, but shall readily sacrifice inferior considerations to the desire of alleviating human misery—Let ladies, then, either lend them child-bed-linen, during the month in which they are confined; or, let them supply them with any old linen, with which they may be able to accommodate them. And let them extend to them that pecuniary aid, which they may then require, and those necessaries and comforts, from which, otherwise, they must be precluded *.

* I must here be permitted to mention a similar method, which has proved extremely beneficial to the objects whom it is intended to relieve, and might be rendered extensively useful. A sufficient quantity of linen is purchased, and lent to each poor married woman during her lying-in; and about half a guinea is given towards defraying her expences.—The fund, by which this institution is supported, is raised by a subscription of 6s. 6d. per quarter; on admission, each subscriber pays 7s. for the purchase of linen, and one quarter in advance; and any poor inhabitant becomes an object of relief, whether a parishioner or not. So that a lying-in charity of this sort may be easily established in any parish, and solicits the attention of the benevolent.

I have

I have often heard the poor speak of this kind of benevolence, as being singularly useful; and have frequently been told, that their condition, from being miserable to the last degree, was rendered comfortable by this timely and judicious relief. It is, therefore, with peculiar pleasure, that this mode of charity is recommended to the attention of those, whose feelings of sympathy are ever ready to commiserate the distresses, and mitigate the hardships, of their fellow-creatures. In such employments, so congenial to the natural tenderness and sensibility of the softer sex, female worth and excellence " have," in part, " their reward" in the present sympathetic feelings of their nature—but, a greater and a better is prepared for them in that future state, where the giving of " a cup of water *," the slightest kind office, rendered to suffering humanity, will neither be forgotten, nor unrewarded.

* St. Matth. x. 42.

RULES

OF A

FRIENDLY SOCIETY*.

With a view to promote benevolence, and to secure mutual relief and support in cases of sickness, accident, or old age, we, whose names are here inserted, agree to the following rules:

I. This society shall consist of a president, two stewards, a clerk, and two assistants, and as

---

* The reader is requested to bear in mind, that the rules are designed for those who constitute the labouring classes of the community; of course, they are adapted, as much as possible, to their sentiments, their habits, their capacities, and their mode of life. As the utility of Friendly Societies depends, in a great measure, on the regulations that are established among them, too much pains cannot be taken to render them as explicit and judicious as possible. The author does not flatter himself with thinking, that the constitution of this society, and the following rules, though formed after mature deliberation, are free from every objection, or will suit every benefit-club, without regard to the number of members, and to their particular circumstances and views. He hopes, however, that they are adapted to the general purposes of these excellent institutions, and may be beneficial among those industrious and useful members of society, for whose advantage they are principally intended. And he takes this opportunity of adding, that he will be much obliged to those, who will suggest any remarks, by which these tracts, or these rules, may be improved.

many members as it may be thought proper to admit; and shall meet, at the house appointed for the purpose, on the first Monday in every month, from seven till nine in the evening, during the summer half-year, and from six till eight, during the winter half-year, when the list shall be called over by the clerk, and all the business relating to the society shall be transacted.

The usual number in Friendly Societies is, perhaps, from sixty to a hundred. But in fixing the number of a benefit-club, attention should be paid to the size and accommodation of the house, where the meetings are to be held. And, to prevent future disputes, it is earnestly recommended to all benefit-societies, to make the rules as judicious as they can, at their first institution; and then, not to alter them on every trifling occasion, as such alterations seldom fail to be attended with dangerous consequences.

II. No person shall be admitted a member of this society, who is not capable of earning one shilling a week more than the allowance paid to sick members; and if it be afterwards proved, that, at the time of his admission, he did not usually earn nine shillings a week, he shall be excluded.

III. Any person, wishing to become a member, is requested to bring or send to the society a certificate of his age, and a proper attestation of his character, signed by his employer, or by two respectable inhabitants of the parish where he resides. When these attestations have been laid before the society, his name, his occupation, and his place of residence, shall be exhibited, in a public manner, in the club-room, till he be ballotted for; and notice shall be given to all the members, that ———— wishes to be admitted, and that his election will come on at the next quarterly meeting.

IV. It is agreed, that all members shall be chosen by ballot; and that no person shall be admitted a member without the consent of three-fourths of the society then present, and who is not in good health, and between eighteen and forty-five years of age.

If any person, on admission, shall produce a false certificate of his age, or character, or have any concealed disorder, and it be afterwards discovered, he shall forfeit all he has paid to the box, and be expelled; and any member who is, or may be, acquainted with such fraud, shall immediately inform the president and stewards, or pay a fine of five shillings.

And it is farther agreed, that every member, under twenty-five years of age, shall pay, on admission, two shillings and sixpence to the fund; between the age of twenty-five and thirty, he shall pay five shillings; and between thirty and thirty-five, ten shillings and sixpence, besides a shilling to the clerk, threepence to the house, and a shilling for the articles. Every person, above the age of thirty-five, shall pay twelve shillings for every year he exceeds that period, besides the ten shillings and sixpence of entrance-money, and fee to the clerk &c.; and none shall be admitted who are above forty-five years of age.

It is found necessary, to make the terms of admission so very moderate, as few would become members, were they required to contribute according to Dr. Price's tables for different ages.

V. The business of this society shall be conducted by the president, the two stewards, the clerk,

clerk, two affiftants, and a Committee, who fhall be chofen in the following manner: The Prefident fhall be elected by ballot at the quarterly meeting, from the lift of fubfcribers. Whoever has the majority of votes fhall ferve as prefident for the enfuing half-year, or forfeit five fhillings, and fhall not be eligible again for the fpace of eighteen months. If he choofe to pay the fine, the perfon who has the next greateft number of votes fhall ferve, or forfeit five fhillings; and the third, &c. fhall be fubject to the fame penalty.

The affiftants fhall ferve as they ftand on the lift of enrolment, or pay five fhillings; and when they refign in rotation, they fhall ferve as ftewards, or forfeit the fame fum.

Both the ftewards and the affiftants fhall continue in office fix months; but thofe who cannot write fhall be excufed from ferving any office, on paying five fhillings each.

The clerk fhall be chofen by a majority of the fociety, and fhall continue in office as long as he does his duty, and keeps the books properly. And the manner of choofing the Committee, with the purpofe for which it is appointed, will be fpecified in the forty-feventh article.

VI. The office of the Prefident is, to regulate the tranfactions, and to limit the expences, of the meetings. He is to examine the accounts of the fociety; to obferve that the ftewards, and other officers, do their duty, and, by their affiftance, to keep the fociety in good order, to demand filence, and to fee the reckoning paid. And if a member apply for relief, he fhall enquire into the caufe and nature of the accident or ficknefs, and, within twenty-four hours after

fuch

such application, shall inform one of the stewards, or forfeit one shilling *.

VII. The office of the stewards is, to receive the admission-money of new members and the monthly contributions; to order silence, to pay the reckoning, and to fine any member, who transgresses the rules of the society. They are, by turns, to see, that the sick are provided with proper means of recovery; to visit them, at least, once every week, if the place of residence be not more than three miles from the club-room, or forfeit a shilling for every neglect; and, if farther, the sick person shall send, once a month, a certificate of his illness, signed according to the annexed form, before he be entitled to any allowance from the society.

All sick members shall be paid by the stewards what is due to them every Saturday before six at night; and, that the president may be acquainted with the number, and state of the sick, a list is to be given to him every week. If neither of the stewards visit the sick, within twenty-four hours after notice has been given to them, if within three miles of the club-room, they shall forfeit one shilling each; and if they do not pay what is due to every sick member on Saturday before six o'clock, they shall forfeit two-pence for every hour they neglect payment, the fine to be put into the box, and given to the sick member.

VIII. The office and duty of the clerk are these: to keep the accounts of the society; to register the name, the profession, and the place of abode, of every new member; and to do all other

---

* See Sir Fred. Eden " on the Poor," in his account of Lancaster.

business, which may be deemed necessary for the order and prosperity of the society. In the course of the last month in every quarter, he is to give timely notice to those members, whose turn it is to serve as assistants, and to receive their answers. Whoever consents to serve, and does neither appear at the meeting, nor substitute another to represent him, when he enters on his office, shall pay a fine of five shillings.

The clerk is also to summon members to funerals, and on other occasions, as the business of the society may require; to take care, that all fines and contributions, and all allowances to every sick member, be kept separately, that they may be easily ascertained. He is to keep an exact account of the several sums of money received and paid every month; and, at the quarterly and annual meetings, he is to lay the accounts before the society.

He is to receive for salary twopence every quarter from every member, to be collected by the stewards: and is not to be discharged, without sufficient reason assigned, and that agreed on by a majority of the society summoned on purpose.

The duties of the clerk have been more particularly specified, as the books of Friendly Societies are seldom kept with sufficient accuracy and perspicuity.

IX. The assistants succeed by rotation; and their duty is to see that the rules of the society be observed, and to give impartially to every member, an equal share of liquor.—To the utmost of their power, they shall detect any member who misbehaves; and, if either of them omit to give in his name, the assistant, who was guilty of the neglect, shall pay the same as the offender.

der.—To promote good order, an affiftant fhall be ftationed at each end of the room, to ferve the members with liquor, and to notice their behaviour.

X. The prefident, the ftewards, the clerk, and the affiftants, who do not come into the clubroom within half an hour after the time appointed for the meeting, fhall forfeit half-a-crown, each; but if any of them, being prevented by illnefs, fhall fend the key, they fhall not be fined.

XI. In cafe of the abfence, illnefs, or death, of the prefident, his powers fhall devolve on the ftewards, by virtue of their office; and they may call in the temporary affiftance of any member, till the next meeting of the fociety.—If either of the ftewards or affiftants be abfent or ill, the next member on the lift fhall officiate for him, till the quarterly meeting, when he fhall begin to do his own duty, if his health will permit.

In the abfence of the clerk, the prefident may appoint a fubftitute; and, on his refignation or death, a general meeting fhall be convened by the prefident and ftewards, and another clerk fhall be chofen by ballot, a week's notice of the time of election being given to the members.

XII. A box fhall be provided with five locks, wherein fhall be depofited the books, and other property of the fociety. Three locks fhall be fixed on the outfide, all of different wards, the keys of which fhall be kept by the ftewards and clerk; one infide-key to be kept by the prefident, and the other by the perfon who gives fecurity for the box. The box fhall not be opened, except in the prefence of the ftewards and clerk, or whom they may appoint; but, if any officer fhall fubftitute another, who already has a

G key,

key, or shall leave the club-room, without seeing the box locked, and the books and property of the society secured, he shall be fined ten shillings and sixpence.

XIII. No persons shall be admitted into the club-room but those who are, or intend to be, members of this society.

XIV. If any member shall belong to any other beneficial society, he shall be excluded from this; but, if he choose to pay a larger contribution every month, while in health, he shall be entitled to a proportionable increase of allowance, when he is sick, lame, or old.

XV. Each member shall pay, at every monthly meeting, one shilling and five-pence into the box, and shall be entitled to three-penny worth of liquor *. But it is agreed that, unless a majority

---

* In those parts of the country, where this contribution might be considered as rather too great to be paid by common labourers, a Friendly Society might be established, the subscription to which might be only one shilling and twopence per month; the shilling for the sick, and the twopence to be spent. In this case an allowance of seven shillings per week, instead of eight, might be made to sick and disabled members. On the other hand, if, in consequence of the advanced price of provisions, the members should wish to receive nine shillings per week during illness, they may be entitled to this sum, by contributing one shilling and fourpence per month to the fund, and threepence to the house.

But *general* tables for settling these payments, and allowances, will not always be correct. Attention should be paid to the age of members, at the time of their admission, to the healthiness of the situation, and to the nature of the manufacture in which the members of the society are chiefly employed. It should also be considered, that some places, and some occupations, are much more healthy than others; and that the inhabitants of great towns are, in general, much shorter-lived than the inhabitants of small towns, and of country parishes. Hence Mr. Baron Mazeres and Dr. Price have calculated distinct tables, according to the probabilities of life in London, and in the country.

of the members be prefent, only three-fourths of the money to the houfe fhall be expended at the monthly meeting; the remainder, if wanted, fhall be applied towards defraying the expences of the annual feaft.

When any of the members happen to have a room fufficiently large, it certainly would be much more comfortable, that the fociety fhould meet there; and the expences incurred at a public houfe would be faved.

XVI. In paying contributions or fines at any time, no member fhall offer more than five-pence half-penny in copper, under the penalty of forfeiting threepence.

XVII. The quarterly meetings fhall be held on the firft club night after Lady-day, Midfummer, Michaelmas, and Chriftmas; and the accounts fhall then be paffed by the prefident and ftewards, and reported to the fociety.

XVIII. On the anniverfary meeting, which fhall be held on the firft Monday in June, unlefs the fociety appoint a different day, the Minifter fhall be requefted to read prayers, and to preach a fermon, at the expence of the fociety; the parifh-clerk to be allowed two fhillings and fixpence.

Every member, who fhall attend the faid meeting at dinner, and does not come into the club-room, at or before half-paft ten o'clock in the forenoon, and walk in an orderly manner to and from church, two and two, according to feniority on the lift, and hear divine fervice, unlefs prevented by ficknefs, fhall forfeit a fhilling.

Each member, not receiving any benefit from the club, or otherwife excufed by the articles, fhall pay two fhillings for dinner and liquor.

Whoever objects to what the president and stewards have provided, shall forfeit a shilling: Dinner on the table at two o'clock. No victuals shall be sent to any person, except to a sick member; and if any irregularities happen, such as embezzling the victuals or liquor, the member, who thus offends, shall be fined half-a-crown. The annual accounts, both in the receipt and expenditure, being first examined and audited by the president and stewards, shall be laid on the table after dinner, for the inspection of the members.

XIX. Every member, within ten miles of the club-room, shall pay his subscriptions and contributions every month, or forfeit threepence; if they are not paid the second month, he shall forfeit sixpence; and if all fines and contributions are not paid at the next quarterly meeting, he shall forfeit a shilling. And it is agreed, that any member, within the said distance, neglecting to pay them on the feast day, or on the monthly meeting before it, shall be excluded. But, if he should afterwards come to the society, and apologize for his repeated neglect, he shall, if he be in good health, be re-admitted, on his paying his arrears and the penalty, though he be superannuated; and, after contributing twelve months more, shall again be entitled to all the advantages of other free members.

XX. If any sick member remove into the country for the benefit of his health, or if any member quit his place of residence, he shall, within a month, inform the president or clerk, where he is removed, or forfeit a shilling; but, before his removal, he shall pay all his arrears to the fund. During sickness, lameness, or blindness, he shall send a certificate, (post paid,) signed by the minister, church-wardens, and

and overseers of the poor, or the majority of them, and by the physician, surgeon, or apothecary, if any attend him, stating his complaint, inclosed in a letter, according to the annexed form, and, from the date thereof, he shall be paid his allowance.

If his residence be more than three miles from the club-room, this attestation, if required, shall be renewed every month, or he shall derive no benefit from the fund. He shall also inform the society, how the allowance is to be remitted to him.—If he remove fifty miles or upwards, he shall be allowed six months to pay his contributions, and, if under fifty and more than ten, he shall be allowed three months. If he fail in the payment of his subscriptions, within the time limited, he shall be excluded. If a member die who resides more than three miles from the club-room, his heirs shall be entitled to the allowance which the articles specify, but the members are not required to attend his funeral.—Any member defrauding, or attempting to defraud, the society, by a false certificate, shall be expelled.

XXI. No member shall receive any benefit from this society, till he has contributed to it for twelve months; after which, if by illness or accident he be rendered incapable of following his usual occupation, he shall send a note to the president, in the form prescribed, and he will then be entitled to eight shillings a week, from the date thereof. When the fund of the society amounts to six hundred pounds, and while it continues above that sum, he shall receive nine shillings per week. But it is agreed, that all fines shall be first deducted out of his weekly allowance.—If his illness continue less than a week, he shall be paid at the rate of one shilling and two-pence per day; but if it be occasioned by quarrelling, drunkenness, or any other disorderly or criminal conduct, he shall, during such illness, derive no benefit from the club.

Members, when recovered from their illness, shall give notice thereof to the president and stewards.

In country villages, where the character and conduct of every particular member are well known, and where impositions are easily detected, it, perhaps, might be advisable to insert such a rule as this: "Any member, when he is recovering from a "fit of illness, and incapable of earning as much "as usual, yet able and willing to do something "towards his support, shall have a weekly allowance, not exceeding four shillings, and not "for more than a month, at the discretion of the "president and stewards, who shall make report "thereof at the quarterly meeting."

XXII. A surgeon and apothecary shall be chosen by the society, to attend the sick and lame members within three miles of the club-room, and a fixed salary shall be paid him for medicine and attendance, to defray which, each member shall contribute one shilling and six-pence to the fund, at the annual meeting.—If any sick or lame member prefer the assistance of any other medical person than the one appointed by the society, he shall pay the expences of his illness himself, but shall not be deprived of the allowance from the club.

Nothing can shew more strikingly, that the public attention has not, hitherto, been sufficiently directed to the encouragement of Friendly Societies, than the injudicious rules by which they are usually regulated. I do not entirely allude to the style, in which their rules

rules are expressed; for, among the lower orders of mankind, elegance of language is not to be expected. But surely, as health is an invaluable blessing to the poor, one would expect, that all Benefit-clubs would have been particularly anxious, that every sick member should be provided with proper medical aid. And yet, among all the rules of Friendly Societies which I have seen, I only recollect one instance relating to this important object; though it is obvious, that amidst the many accidents to which the poor are peculiarly exposed, such a rule as is here proposed, seems to be essentially necessary. Indeed, a society, instituted for no other purpose than that of paying for medical assistance would be of great utility. I can, however, easily suppose, that, in some benefit-clubs, the funds will not admit of it. But among other beneficial effects which the poor enjoy, by having medical advice at their own houses, they are taught the advantages of cleanliness, and of well-ventilated rooms. They may also be recommended to the attention of the charitable and opulent in their neighbourhood, and thereby may receive those necessaries and comforts, which will essentially contribute to their recovery.

XXIII. If any member should be found begging, or soliciting charity, while he receives benefit from the society, and it can be proved by two credible witnesses, he shall forfeit ten shillings and sixpence.

XXIV. If any member, during the time he receives the benefit of the club, be found at work, or seen drunk, or gaming at any public house, he shall be expelled; and if he be not at home, by four o'clock in winter, and seven in summer, he shall forfeit five shillings: and any member who knows the same, and does not mention it at the next meeting, shall forfeit five shillings.

XXV. Any member happening to be ill, before he be entitled to any allowance, shall not be required to contribute his usual payments, during sickness or incapacity to work; nor shall he be fined for not serving any office. In all such cases, he shall be considered as an object, claiming the commiseration of every individual in the society.

XXVI. If a member, on the night of his admission, choose to pay one year's contribution to the fund, in addition to his entrance-money, &c. he shall be entitled to, and enjoy, the privileges of other free members.

XXVII. At the anniversary meeting, on the entrance of the president, &c. into office, and on the admission of new members, the articles shall be read publicly by the clerk. The new member shall then subscribe them; and the annexed declaration shall be made in the presence of the society.

XXVIII. It is agreed, that none shall be admitted, whose occupations are peculiarly prejudicial to health, or exposed to unusual casualties, such as painters, miners, brass-founders, workers in white lead, soldiers, and sailors; and whoever shall belong to any of these professions shall be excluded.

XXIX. If any member voluntarily enlist into the army or navy, or be in any way employed in the sea-service, or if he quit the kingdom of Great Britain for more than three months, he shall be excluded. But, if he should be impressed, he shall be exempted from any farther payments to the fund till he be discharged; and then, if he be free from lameness and disease, he shall be entitled to the same privileges as before, on paying his next subscription, within three months after his discharge.

If he be wounded or difabled in his Majefty's fervice, the allowance, which he had received at different times from the fund, during illnefs, fhall be deducted from his monthly contributions; and the balance, if any, fhall be paid to him; and he fhall be excluded.

XXX. If any member, or members, fhall be drawn for the militia, the money for paying a fubftitute, or fubftitutes, fhall be advanced from the fund; and every member of this fociety, who was liable to be drawn, fhall pay by inftalments fixpence a month, till the whole be repaid.

XXXI. If any member be arrefted or imprifoned for debt, he fhall be exempted from all payments, but fhall not receive any benefit from the fund during his confinement. When he is difcharged, he fhall not be called on to pay arrears; and if he die in prifon, the fame allowance fhall be given as to others; the members, however, fhall not be obliged to attend his funeral.—But, if he be caft into prifon, and convicted of felony, or of any fraudulent or difhoneft tranfaction, he fhall be excluded from any benefit which otherwife might have accrued to him from the fociety.

XXXII. The landlord fhall accommodate the fociety with a club-room, and fhall provide pens, ink, fire, and candles. He fhall alfo give fecurity for the box, and for any other property with which he fhall be entrufted.—At every quarterly meeting, there fhall be depofited in his hands the fum of five pounds, to enable the prefident and ftewards to pay the weekly allowance to fick members.

When the ftock fhall amount to a larger fum than the immediate exigences of the fociety may require, it fhall be placed out at intereft on

landed

landed security, or in some of the public funds, and vested in the names of some neighbouring gentlemen, chosen by the majority of members, in trust for the society; and such trustees shall give security for the faithful appropriation, both of principal and interest, to the purposes of the society.

That Friendly Societies should be jealous of any interference, in the management of their own property, is not to be wondered at. This jealousy, however, has been carried to such an excess, as to have proved fatal to some of them. Apprehensive that a law might be enacted, which would either affect them, or their property, some societies have preferred private security, and entrusted their money into the hands of persons, where it became insecure; and others, elated with the idea of having a club-estate, have made such impolitic purchases of land, or of houses, that the sick members could not receive that relief which the articles had prescribed.—The above rule is intended to prevent any disappointment of this sort.

XXXIII. When the fund of this society shall amount to upwards of two hundred pounds, the sum of six pounds may be lent to any member who has contributed for five years, to help him to purchase a cow; on condition, that he give a promissory note, signed by himself and two housekeepers, to be approved of by the president and stewards, for the repayment of the said sum, with interest, by instalments, of at least five shillings per month.

XXXIV. If any member leave money with the landlord, to pay his contributions, and they are not paid, at the next meeting of the society, the landlord shall be fined sixpence; or, if any member receive money of another member, and he neglect

neglect to give it to the stewards, the same penalty shall be incurred. If a member should be excluded by any such omission, he shall be re-admitted.

XXXV. The society shall not be removed from the place where it is now held without cause, judged to be sufficient by a majority of members summoned for that purpose; and if any member propose the removal of the society, without assigning a sufficient reason, he shall pay five shillings.

XXXVI. It is agreed, that this society shall not be dissolved so long as any three members are willing to support it: and any member, proposing to break up the society, or to divide the money, shall be expelled.

XXXVII. If any sick or disabled member have received a weekly allowance for twelve successive months, without intermission, his allowance shall be reduced to four shillings per week; but, if blind, or he be totally confined to his bed, he shall continue to receive his full pay of eight shillings per week.—If he recover his health, and be able to follow his usual occupation, he shall pay the same contributions as other members.—If it be proved, that he earns, on an average, five shillings a-week, he shall be excluded; and, if any member be reduced to half-pay, each member, while the fund is under two hundred pounds, shall contribute to it twopence per month extraordinary.

XXXVIII. If any member be suspected to impose on the society, by feigning lameness or sickness, the president and stewards shall be empowered to call in a physician, surgeon, or apothecary, to examine him; and if, in the judgment of the physician, surgeon, or apothecary, it appears to be a fraud and imposition on the society, he shall be tried by a Committee, according to the forty-seventh article. If he refuse to be examined, he shall be deemed guilty, and expelled: the expence of examination to be paid out of the fund. And if any sick member send notice, that he is able to resume his usual business, with a view to evade the reduction of the weekly allowance, he not being recovered from the infirmity with which he was afflicted, such member, on the evidence of a physician, surgeon, or apothecary, shall be deemed an impostor, and tried by a committee; and their determination shall be final.

XXXIX. If a free member remove more than twenty miles from the parish where the club is kept, and find a Friendly Society established in the neighbourhood where he is settled willing to admit him, the allowance, which he had received at different times from the fund during illness, shall be deducted from his monthly contributions; and the balance, if any, shall be returned to him, if he choose it, on the president's receiving from the clerk of such society an intimation that they will allow him to become a member.

Were Friendly Societies to become general, Dr. Price, in his Appendix to his second volume on Reversionary Payments, has formed some useful tables, shewing the sums payable to members at removals, in proportion to their age and contributions.

XL. It is hereby enjoined, that members at the club shall always behave with decency and civility to each other; and particularly to the president, stewards, clerk, and assistants, shewing proper respect to their offices; or they shall forfeit twopence.

LXI.

XLI. Every member, on his coming into the club-room, fhall take his feat, and not walk about the room, or make a noife, or fit before the fire, to the inconvenience of other members. Whoever refufes to take his feat, when ordered by the prefident, ftewards, affiftants, or clerk, fhall pay threepence for the firft offence, fixpence for the fecond, a fhilling for the third, and half a crown for the fourth.

XLII. With a view to promote peace and good manners at all our meetings, and to guard againft diffenfions and immoral conduct, it is agreed that, if any member come into the room where the fociety meets, and fhall curfe, fwear, or utter any profane or abufive language, or fhall offer to lay wagers, or promote gaming; if he be intoxicated, or raife any quarrel, or challenge another to work, or depreciate his knowledge of his bufinefs; for every fuch offence, he fhall forfeit fixpence : and if any of the officers be guilty of any of thefe offences, they fhall pay a fhilling.

XLIII. To prevent confufion, it is alfo agreed, that, during any debate, only one perfon fhall be permitted to fpeak at a time: and he fhall addrefs himfelf to the prefident. If any two or more endeavour to fpeak, the prefident fhall determine who is to be heard firft; and whoever interrupts the fpeaker fhall forfeit fixpence.—Any member refufing to keep filence, when enjoined by the prefident, fhall forfeit a fhilling.

XLIV. If any member be guilty of uttering or promoting any feditious language in the club-room, on the evidence of two witneffes, he fhall be fined ten fhillings and fixpence, to be paid at the next meeting.

XLV.

XLV. It is agreed, that every subject of conversation, having a tendency to create dissensions in the society, or to be subversive of harmony and good order, shall be carefully avoided. Any member, therefore, who enters into religious or political disputes with his neighbour, shall forfeit, for the first offence, sixpence; for the second offence, in the same evening, a shilling; if he still endeavour to disturb the harmony and good humour of the society, he shall pay, for the third offence, half-a-crown; and, for the fourth offence, he shall be excluded.

XLVI. It is farther agreed, that none shall order silence, but the officers or clerk; and if any member call for liquor or tobacco, without leave of the president or assistants, he shall pay for it himself, and forfeit sixpence. No more ale, beer, or any spirituous liquor whatever, shall be drank or called for, than the fifteenth article prescribes. If any be ordered, the assistants shall pay for it out of their own pockets.

By these rules, thus enforced, the chief objections that can be urged against Friendly Societies are removed: when properly regulated and conducted, they neither promote intemperance, nor encourage political debates.

XLVII. As it will be difficult, if not impossible, by any general rules, to meet every case that may occur, it is hereby agreed, that, if any dispute arise, which cannot be determined by the articles, it shall be submitted, at the quarterly meeting, to the arbitration of a Committee. To guard against secret animosities, the committee shall always vote by ballot, and shall consist of eleven members*;

---

* The act, which passed in 1793, for the encouragement of Friendly Societies, requires that eleven, at least, shall constitute a Committee.

six chosen by the society who are not in office, four by the stewards and assistants, each nominating one, and the president of the society for the time, in virtue of his office. If any member think himself aggrieved by their verdict, he may appeal to the next quarterly meeting, when another committee shall be chosen; but, if the decision of the former committee be then confirmed, the member or members, thus convicted, shall pay double the award.

All honorary members, who annually subscribe one guinea or upwards, and who happen to be in the club-room, shall be on committees; and previous notice shall be sent to them, by the clerk, of the business to be taken into consideration.

In adjusting differences, it will be particularly useful to have the advice of well-informed minds.

XLVIII. A list of the honorary members shall be placed, from gratitude and respect, in the club-room.

XLIX. If the president or stewards embezzle any of the money, with which they are entrusted for the relief of sick members, or for other purposes, he or they, so offending, shall be expelled the society, and prosecuted as the law directs.

L. If the stewards collect bad money, they shall make it good; and any member offering bad money to the stewards shall pay sixpence.

LI. No part of the fund, raised by this society, shall ever be laid out in the purchase of lottery tickets; and every member, who has had any share in the lottery, or in any other game of chance, since he became a member of this club, shall pay a fine of ten shilling and sixpence.

This article is highly necessary, as every species of gambling proves ruinous to the comfort and morals of the poor, as well as of the rich; and is productive of idleness, poverty, domestic misery, and inevitable ruin.

LII. Any member upbraiding another for having received from the fund any benefit, to which he was entitled, shall, on the evidence of two witnesses, forfeit a shilling; and if he accuse a member of a breach of any of the articles, and cannot prove his assertion, he shall also pay a shilling.

LIII. If any of the society, or the landlord, pay the arrears of any member, with a view to save him from expulsion, the clerk shall give the earliest notice thereof to the said member; and, if he does not repay him, at or before the next meeting, the money shall be returned to the person who advanced it, and the member shall be expelled.

Any member attending the society, and not paying his contributions before he leave it, shall forfeit three-pence.

LIV. It is agreed, that these rules shall be observed by the members, while they continue in the club-room, even after the club-hours; and whoever obstructs the clerk, or any of the officers, in settling their business, shall forfeit a shilling.

LV. The president, stewards, and clerk, when they resign their respective offices, shall give up the money, books, and accounts, to their successors; if there be any deficiencies, they shall be made good by them.

LVI. To promote these our benevolent intentions towards each other, and to prevent the box from ever being shut against any sick or disabled member, it is agreed, that, if the fund of this society should be reduced, at any future period,

to

to a hundred pounds or under, each member, not indispofed, shall contribute two-pence extraordinary a week towards the support of the club. So that the sum of eight shillings per week shall not be withheld from such sick, lame, or blind members, as are entitled to receive the same; nor is the money, for the payment of funeral-expences, ever to be discontinued.

LVII. The wife of a free member, having more than two children, under fourteen years of age, shall be entitled to ten shillings and sixpence from the society every time she lies-in, on producing a certificate of their marriage; and every free member, having a wife and two or more children whom he supports, shall, on the death of every child, receive ten shillings and sixpence towards the funeral-expences. And in such cases each member shall pay two-pence extra at the next monthly meeting.

This rule is made with a view to meet contingent expences. The contributions of individuals should be proportionable to the number of the members.

LVIII. If any member, being sick or lame, wish to be admitted into an hospital, the president and stewards shall deposit whatever sum may be requisite for his admission; and the money, so advanced, shall be returned to the society by the sick or lame member when he is discharged, or he shall forfeit double the sum.

And it is agreed, that a free member shall be allowed six shillings for himself and family, while he is in the hospital; and, if he should die there, the stewards shall see that he be decently interred: any necessary expences, incurred by the stewards, to be deducted from the allowance due to his representatives.

LIX. The president and stewards shall not be entitled to any compensation from the society for any trouble, or loss of time, they may sustain in the discharge of the duties of their office; but all necessary expences shall be repaid them every month. And, if any dispute shall arise in settling this allowance, it shall be decided by a Committee, chosen according to the forty-seventh article.

LX. If any member of this society shall be inoculated for the small-pox, or shall catch the infection in the natural way, he shall receive the usual allowance, while he is afflicted with it; but, if he die in consequence, only two pounds shall be given by the society towards defraying the expences of his funeral, each member to contribute nine-pence. And it is agreed, that all members, who have not had the small-pox themselves, or who have families of young children, shall not be obliged to attend.—If the child of a member be inoculated, and it should die, there shall be an allowance made of five shillings towards the funeral; but, if the child take the infection naturally, no allowance shall be given.

This is offered as a means of encouraging inoculation among the lower orders.

LXI. While the fund of the society amounts to two hundred pounds, any member, upwards of seventy years of age, shall receive an annuity of three shillings per week: and upwards of seventy-five, of four shillings per week, with the privilege of earning what he can for his further support; the members contributing two-pence a month to the fund.

LXII. On the death of a member, or of a free member's wife, it shall be the duty of the president and stewards to see, that the corpse be
interred

interred in a decent manner, and that a sufficient sum, out of the money allowed by the society, be appropriated to the payment of the funeral-expences.—The minister shall have the earliest notice of the death of every member, and shall be requested to preach a sermon, for which he shall be paid by the society *.

When any member dies, the society shall meet, at the time appointed, at the club-room, or at the nearest and most convenient public-house, as the president shall direct, to proceed from thence to the house where the deceased lieth, to attend the funeral to the grave. Each member is to provide himself with hatband and gloves, at his own expence.—The clerk shall write out a list for the stewards and assistants, who shall give the earliest notice to each member of the time and place of meeting; and whoever neglects to attend, unless he be indisposed, or resides upwards of four miles from the spot, shall forfeit two shillings and sixpence.

At every funeral, the members are to spend threepence each, at the house where they meet. But it is agreed, that, when a member dies of a putrid fever, only the bearers shall be required to attend: and no sermon shall be preached. *This is intended to prevent infectious disorders from spreading.*

* In some societies, only the officers, and about six members, who take it in rotation, attend funerals. But it may be here observed, that, as these funerals are generally in the evening, they do not interrupt the usual occupations of the members. And, when the societies desire (as they do at Sunbury), that a sermon may be preached, the minister will hardly refuse, for many go to church on these occasions who are irregular in their attendance at other times; and he has an opportunity of directing their attention to some awful and momentous topic, when the mind is more than usually open to receive serious impressions.

LXIII. It is agreed, that the six youngest members on the roll of the society shall carry the corpse of a deceased member to the place of interment; whoever refuses, if he be not on the sick list, shall pay two shillings and sixpence.

LXIV. And it is further agreed, that, if a member die before he has subscribed twelve months to the fund, two pounds shall be allowed towards his funeral-expences; each member contributing nine-pence to the box at the next meeting. And, at the decease of a free member, five pounds shall be paid to his widow, children, or representative, on the next club-night after the funeral; or two pounds before, if required, to defray the expences; and every member shall pay one shilling and sixpence to the fund at or before the next quarterly meeting.

LXV. At the death of a free member's wife, he shall receive two pounds to defray the funeral-expences, and each member shall contribute nine-pence to the fund; but this allowance shall not be paid by the society to any individual more than once.

LXVI. When any member's wife dies, a certificate of their marriage shall be produced before any money be paid by the president and stewards towards the funeral-expences.

Where a society is principally instituted for the benefit of widows, it would be proper to make a rule to this effect: " *If the widow of any member shall live a* " *profligate life, or shall have an illegitimate child,* " *she shall be excluded from every future benefit of* " *this society.*"

LXVII. When a member has been burdensome to the society by long illness, and has received more money from the fund than he ever contributed

contributed to it, only two pounds shall be allowed towards his funeral; and each member shall pay nine-pence.

The large sums, which are generally paid on the death of members, and of members wives, seem to drain the funds of Friendly Societies too much.

LXVIII. If any member commit self-murder, the other members shall not be required to attend his funeral; and only one pound shall be given towards the expences.—And, if a member should happen to die in a parish work-house, no money shall be paid by the society to defray his funeral-expences.

LXIX. It is here agreed, that all fines and forfeits shall be put into the box.

LXX. It is also agreed, that these Rules shall be exhibited at the next general quarter-sessions of the county, to be examined, allowed, and confirmed, by the justices, according to the provisions of the Act of Parliament, passed for the relief and encouragement of Friendly Societies, in order to be entitled to that security and those advantages held out to us by the Legislature *.

* 33 Geo. III. chap. 54.
One advantage, arising from having the rules confirmed, and deposited with the clerk of the peace, is, that, if any person, intrusted with any property belonging to the society, shall become a bankrupt, or insolvent, the money due to the society shall be paid before any other debts.—Besides this, if the trustees or officers refuse to deliver their accounts, and to pay the balance to the society, application may be made to the Court of Chancery, where, by the terms of the act, no fee shall be taken.—Bonds are not chargeable with any stamp-duty. And no fee is allowed to the clerk of the peace for registering the rules.

LXXI.

LXXI. Every member shall purchase a printed copy of these articles, for which he shall pay a shilling.

LXXII. Whoever refuses to pay the forfeits, which the foregoing rules impose, or will not comply with the laws and regulations of the society, shall be expelled.

LXXIII. The society, whenever three-fourths of the members shall deem it necessary, shall alter, amend, or repeal, any of these rules. But no rule, order, or regulation, shall be altered, rescinded, or repealed, unless at a general meeting of the society, convened by public notice, in writing, signed by the clerk, in pursuance of a requisition for that purpose by three-fourths of the members then present, and publicly read at the two monthly meetings to be held next before the quarterly meeting for such alteration or repeal,—unless a Committee shall have been nominated for that purpose, in which case the Committee shall be convened in like manner, with the concurrence and approbation of three-fourths of the members then present, or by the same proportion of the Committee; and such alteration or repeal shall be subject to the review of the justices at the quarter-sessions, and shall be filed with the rolls of the sessions: provided, however, that no alteration shall be made, which tends to dissolve the society, and affects the thirty-sixth article.

LXXIV. If it should be thought requisite, at any time, to make any additional article, before it shall be valid, it shall first be proposed at a public meeting, and, if approved of by a majority of the members then present, a copy of the article shall be written by the clerk, and given

given to the stewards and assistants to be sent by them to all the members, that they may have time to consider the propriety of admitting or rejecting it. And if, at the next quarterly meeting, the said article be ratified and approved of by a majority of the members then present, it shall be entered by the clerk among the other articles and regulations of the society; and as soon as confirmed by the justices become binding on the members.

LXXV. In conclusion, it is earnestly recommended to all the members of this society, to lead a life of piety and virtue, to cultivate a benevolent intercourse with each other, and faithfully to observe the rules that are here established.

THESE RULES, with the following forms, were this day agreed on by the unanimous consent of the members. In witness whereof we have hereunto subscribed our names.

Forms and Certificates to be observed:

1st. A certificate of age, to be required of every person at the time of his admission; and, 2dly, of character, from his employer, or from two respectable inhabitants of the parish where he resides, in the following manner:

" This is to certify, from our own personal
" knowledge of the life and behaviour of ———,
" that he is sober, honest, healthy, peaceable, and
" industrious."

Notice to be sent by the clerk, when any person is proposed to be a member:

" You are desired to attend at the next quar-
" terly meeting, as ——————— (here mention his
" name, occupation, and place of residence,) is
" proposed to be a member of our society, and
" will then be ballotted for."

Form of notice to be sent to the president by a sick member:

" I hereby declare, that I am so much indis-
" posed, that I am incapable of following my
" usual employment."
(the date)   (signed).

Form of a certificate from a diſtant member claiming relief:

"I hereby declare, that I am ſo much indiſ-
"poſed, (here mention the complaint,) that I
"am incapable of working at my uſual occu-
"pation." (ſigned).
"We whoſe names are hereunto ſubſcribed be-
"lieve the above to be true.
"Miniſter, Church-warden, Overſeer.
"Phyſician, Surgeon, Apothecary."
(the date)

Notice to the preſident from a member who has been ill:

"I hereby inform you, that I am now ſo far
"recovered as to be able to be employed in my
"uſual buſineſs."
(the date) (ſigned).
N. B. If a member cannot write, a verbal notice ſhall be ſufficient.

Form of a certificate to be ſent, on the death of a diſtant member, or his wife:

"This is to certify, that —— died on the
"(here inſert the date).
"Miniſter."

The preſident's declaration at the time of his admiſſion into office:

"I ſolemnly declare and promiſe, that I will
"faithfully execute the office of preſident, and
"with the utmoſt impartiality will diſcharge the
"truſt

" truſt repoſed in me, according to the articles,
" in managing the funds, and conducting the
" buſineſs of this ſociety."

The ſteward's declaration:

" I ſolemnly declare and promiſe, that I will
" faithfully execute the office of ſteward, and
" will, to the beſt of my ability, diſcharge the
" truſt repoſed in me, according to the rules of
" this ſociety."

The aſſiſtant's declaration:

" I ſolemnly declare and promiſe, that I will
" endeavour to detect any member, who behaves
" contrary to the articles, and will impartially
" diſtribute the liquor committed to my care."

The clerk's declaration:

" I ſolemnly declare and promiſe, that I will
" faithfully execute the office of clerk, and will
" keep the books and accompts of this ſociety, with
" as great accuracy and impartiality as I am able."

Declaration to be made by every member, on admiſſion into the ſociety:

" I ſolemnly declare, that I am not, to the
" beſt of my knowledge, above the age of
" ———, nor under the age of eighteen;—that
" I am in good health, and have not any concealed
" diſtemper or infirmity;—that I will endeavour,
" at all times, to promote the peace and pro-
" ſperity, and conform to the rules and orders,
" of this ſociety;—and, if I ſhould be excluded,
" I

"I will resign my claim to any property belonging to this club.

"And I further promise, that I will not apply for relief, except in cases of sickness, accident, inability to work, or old age; and, if I should be obliged to have recourse to the funds of this society for support, I will use every means in my power to recover my health, and, as soon as I am capable of resuming my usual business, will immediately inform the president and stewards."

Declaration to be made by members incapacitated by sickness or age:

"I solemnly declare, that I am incapable, by honest means, of earning five shillings a week; and I hereby promise that, as soon as my health will permit, I will inform the president and stewards, and, when able to follow my usual occupation, will not apply for any further relief from the funds of the society."

IT will be only neceffary to add, that thefe rules, which are defigned for the *general* ftate of labourers, may be eafily varied, fo as to be accommodated to the particular circumftances and local fituation of any rank in fociety. The tradefman, the artift, and the manufacturer, whofe earnings are confiderably greater, may augment their payments into the fund, and thereby be entitled to a proportionable increafe of allowance. But for further particulars of plans, for enabling farmers, mechanics, and tradefmen, as well as the labouring poor, to fecure a comfortable fupport for themfelves, in ficknefs and old age, proportioned to their weekly or quarterly contributions, the reader is referred to two valuable works; to Dr. Price's Treatife on Reverfionary Payments, the 5th edition; and to Mr. Baron Mazeres, on the Doctrine of Life-Annuities. If Friendly Societies fhould ever be eftablifhed in every parifh by voluntary affociations, their tables would be found to be of the greateft utility and importance.

INDEX.

INDEX TO THE RULES.

I. Number of members—Times and place of meeting—Precaution to Friendly Societies.

II. Weekly earnings of perſons, wiſhing to become members.

III. Forms of admiſſion—Certificate of age—Atteſtation of character—Name, occupation, and place of reſidence, publicly exhibited—Notice of the time of election.

IV. Manner of chooſing members—Number of votes, ſtate of health, and age, for admiſſion—Penalty for producing falſe certificate of age, or of character—Ditto, for concealing infirmities—Members privy to ſuch frauds—Terms of admiſſion.

V. Officers of the ſociety:—Time and manner of their election, and their duration in office—Their fines for not ſerving—Who are exempted, and on what condition.

VI. Preſident, his office and duty.

VII. Stewards:—Their duty to receive contributions, viſit ſick members, pay weekly allowance, &c.—Penalty for neglect.

VIII. Clerk, his duty and ſalary—Not to be diſcharged without ſufficient reaſon.

IX. Aſſiſtants, their duty.

X. Officers and clerk, their fine for abſence.

XI. Who

XI. Who officiates, in case of their absence, illness, or death—Death, or resignation of the clerk.

XII. Box to be provided—Books and other property deposited in it—Who shall be entrusted with a key—Officers to see the property of the society secured—Penalty for neglect.

XIII. Who may be admitted into the club-room.

XIV. Members, not to belong to another beneficial society—Their allowance in sickness, proportioned to their contributions in health.

XV. Monthly meetings—Payments at ditto—Expences limited—General tables for settling payments and allowances, not always correct—Reasons assigned.

XVI. Members to bring silver.

XVII. Quarterly meetings, when held—Accounts audited.

XVIII. Anniversary meeting, when and how observed—Procession to church, &c.—Contributions to the dinner—Victuals not to be sent, except to sick members—Irregularities punished—Annual accounts laid before the society.

XIX. Members, within ten miles, to pay subscriptions every [month—Fines for neglect—Arrears to be paid, at or before the annual meeting—On what condition a member, who has been excluded for neglect of payments, may be re-admitted.

XX. Members removing—During sickness, or lameness, to send certificates, properly attested—Time allowed to distant members for payment of contributions — Distant members dying — Attempts to defraud the society by false certificates, how punished.

XXI. How

XXI. How long a member muſt contribute to the fund before he be entitled to relief—Weekly allowance to ſick members—When it may be increaſed—Arrears to be firſt deducted—Member's illneſs, leſs than a week—Illneſs occaſioned by diſorderly or criminal conduct—Members, when recovered, to give notice—On the limited power of the preſident and ſtewards to give temporary relief to members recovering.

XXII. Surgeon and apothecary to attend ſick or lame members—How paid—Remark on the beneficial effects which the poor enjoy, by having medical aſſiſtance at their own houſes.

XXIII. Sick members, not allowed to beg.

XXIV. Ditto, found at work, ſeen intoxicated, gaming, or not at home at night,—the penalty.

XXV. Sick members, not required to contribute, nor to ſerve any office.

XXVI. Members paying a year's contribution on admiſſion,—their privileges.

XXVII. Articles, when read and ſubſcribed— Declaration to be made by the officers and new members.

XXVIII. Perſons, whoſe occupations are peculiarly dangerous or unhealthy, not to be admitted—Members belonging to ſuch employments.

XXIX. Members enliſting into the army or navy—Ditto, impreſſed—Ditto, wounded or diſabled in his Majeſty's ſervice.

XXX. Members drawn for the militia—Subſtitutes, how provided.

XXXI. Members arreſted, or impriſoned for debt—Guilty of felony; or of any fraudulent tranſaction.

XXXII. Landlord's duty—Sum depoſited in his hands—Money belonging to the ſociety, how

I   laid

laid out—Interest, how applied—Trustees to be chosen, and security given—Causes which have proved fatal to some Friendly Societies, and prevented their sick members from receiving relief—Remedy suggested.

XXXIII. Money, how and when lent to any member, for purchasing a cow.

XXXIV. Landlord, or members, neglecting to pay money intrusted to them, &c.

XXXV. Society not to be removed without reason.

XXXVI. Society not to be dissolved, nor the property divided—Penalty for proposing it.

XXXVII. Allowance to members, after one year's illness without intermission—Ditto, when blind, or confined to bed—Members recovered—Earnings of members reduced to half-pay—Contributions to the fund for such members.

XXXVIII. Impositions, by feigning illness, how detected and punished—Ditto, for evading the reduction of allowance—Members refusing to be examined, &c.

XXXIX. Distant members, wishing to be admitted into another Friendly Society—Sum payable at removal—Utility of Dr. Price's tables.

XL. Behaviour to each other in the club-room.

XLI. Members to keep their seats, &c.

XLII. Not to utter profane or abusive language—Members drunk—Wagers, gaming, or quarrelling, not allowed; fines for ditto—Officers guilty of these offences.

XLIII. Members, how to debate—President's power and duty in maintaining order—Forfeit for interrupting the speaker—Ditto, for refusing to be silent, when enjoined by the president.

XLIV. Members uttering or promoting seditious language.

XLV. Reli-

XLV. Religious or political difputes, how punifhed.

XLVI. Who may order filence, or call for liquor—Further regulations to enforce fobriety and good order—Chief objections to Friendly Societies removed.

XLVII. Difputes, not determined by the articles, how and when fettled—Committee, how chofen—Of what number to confift—Manner of voting—Members aggrieved, how to receive redrefs—Honorary members on Committees.

XLVIII. Lift of honorary members to be placed in the club-room.

XLIX. Prefident and ftewards, not to embezzle the property of the fociety.

L. Stewards collecting, or members offering, bad money.

LI. Money belonging to the fociety, not to be laid out in lottery-tickets—Members having a fhare in lotteries—Remark on their baneful effects.

LII. Members not to upbraid each other.

LIII. Money advanced to prevent the expulfion of a member—Fine for attending meetings, and not paying contributions.

LIV. Rules to be obferved after club-hours—Members obftructing the clerk or officers in fettling their bufinefs.

LV. Officers, on refignation, to give an account of money, &c.

LVI. Extra contributions, when the ftate of the fund renders them neceffary.

LVII. Allowance, in certain cafes, to free members wives, on their lying-in; and on the death of a child—Contributions of members.

LVIII. Sick or lame members, admitted into an hofpital—Money depofited—Weekly allowance—Duty of ftewards—Expences incurred.

I   LIX. Officers,

LIX. Officers, not entitled to any compenfation for trouble, or lofs of time—Neceffary expences allowed—Difputes arifing from thence, how fettled.

LX. Members inoculated for the fmall-pox—Catching the diforder naturally; or dying—Allowance—Members, who have not had the fmallpox themfelves, or who have young children, not required to attend funerals—Members dying of that diforder—Children dying under inoculation.

LXI. Members upwards of feventy years of age, their annuity and privileges—Ditto, upwards of feventy-five—Contributions of other members to the fund.

LXII. Duty of prefident and ftewards at funerals—Members to attend—Notice of time and place of meeting—Forfeit for abfence—Expences —Members dying of a putrid fever, &c.

LXIII. Who fhall carry the corpfe of a deceafed member—Fine for refufing.

LXIV. Sums payable on the death of members—Allowance to widows and orphans, &c.— Contributions of other members.

LXV. Allowance, on the death of a free member's wife—Not payable more than once—Contributions.

LXVI. Certificate of marriage, when a member's wife dies—Hint to focieties, inftituted for the benefit of widows.

LXVII. Members burdenfome to the fociety,— the allowance, and contributions, towards their funerals.

LXVIII. Members committing fuicide—Dying in a parifh-workhoufe.

LXIX. Forfeits to be put into the box.

LXX. Rules to be exhibited at the Quarter-Seffions—Advantages ftated.

LXXI. Copy

LXXI. Copy of the articles to be purchased by every member.

LXXII. Members refusing to pay forfeits, or to comply with the rules of the society.

LXXIII. The society may alter or amend rules—No rule to be altered or rescinded, unless at a general meeting, convened by public notice—Forms to be observed, before such alteration or repeal be binding—No alteration to be made, tending to dissolve the society.

LXXIV. Additional articles, how and when proposed and confirmed—Copy to be sent to all the members.

LXXV. Concluding exhortation.

Forms and Certificates, &c.

THE END.

ERRATA.

Page 29. line 19. *for* ar *read* far.
    99.   6. *read* happen.

www.ingramcontent.com/pod-product-compliance
Lightning Source LLC
Chambersburg PA
CBHW021938160426
43195CB00011B/1133